"*Forsaken God?* is a must-read book! Janet skillfully points the reader to specific ways we can remember the goodness of God. This book poignantly weaves biblical wisdom with the true stories of people who have rediscovered the power of honoring, praising, and celebrating God. The bonus in the last few chapters offers hands-on steps for fostering a generation of people who choose to remember the praiseworthy deeds of our God and will pass that knowledge on to others. This is a book you will refer to again and again."

—**Carol Kent,** speaker and author of *When I Lay My Isaac Down*

"This book does a great job of challenging us to share our spiritual journey with our children, grandchildren, and future generations in verbal stories and/or in print. Our stories of how we have experienced God working in and through our lives can have a great impact on future generations of his faithfulness in our lives. We can demonstrate to them that life is hard, not always fair, but God will walk with us if we allow him to hold our hand."

—**Lillian Penner,** National Prayer coordinator, Christian Grandparenting Network, author of *Grandparenting with a Purpose*

"Janet Thompson reminds us we are in a love relationship with our creator. He adores us and wants to shower us with proof. It is we who too often pull away. *Forsaken God?* isn't a book propagating guilt, it is a how-to manual showing us practical as well as spiritual ways to restore the romance in our relationship with the Almighty."

—**Anita Agers Brooks,** inspirational business/life coach, international speaker, and award-winning author of *Getting Through What You Can't Get Over* and *First Hired, Last Fired: How to Become Irreplaceable in Any Job Market*

"In Janet Thompson's *Forsaken God?* you will find a nugget or a boulder that will remind you why you trust in God. Her powerful book will supply more biblical principles, stories, prayers, and discussion ideas than you ever thought possible. I guarantee you will remember!"

—**Kathy Collard Miller,** speaker and author of many books, including *Never Ever Be the Same: A New You Starts Today*

"Janet Thompson has written a book that is greatly needed in our day and age. She expertly and sensitively takes us on a journey to truly consider God and his faithful intervention in our lives, for our good. Each chapter is set up to help the reader consider and contrast his/her present understanding, grow in knowledge and conviction, then apply the truths presented to enjoy a life of faith. Recognizing, honoring, praising, and celebrating God, as this book helps us do, are certain to restore hope and optimism, sorely needed in these days of increasing wickedness. Written for either personal or group study, this book has the potential to transform our generation and many generations to follow."

—**Pamela Christian**, author of the Faith to Live By series, speaker, and media personality: Pamela Christian Ministries

"Janet doesn't just tell us why we should remember God's goodness; she takes us by the hand and guides us through practical ways to recognize God's presence and activity. She helps us develop a new awareness and equips us with the tools we need to step into a new level in our relationship with God. Steeped in Scripture and filled with real life examples, *Forsaken God?* will help you grasp God's goodness and share the bounty!"

—**Kathy Howard**, Bible teacher and author of *Unshakeable Faith* and *God Is My Refuge*

"What a refreshing book! Janet gently guides her readers in remembering the goodness of God when our society has largely forgotten him. The promptings for personal reflection at the end of each chapter help you develop healthy heart habits. Thank you, Janet, for giving us what we need—not another self-help book, but a well-timed reminder of profound truth: God is good."

—**Jocelyn Green**, author of *Faith Deployed*

"When we forget the goodness of God, we lose. When we dwell in the goodness of God, we win. The strength of our lives rises and falls with our accurate view of God. Janet helps us remember God; and in remembering, we become better people who can create a better, more God-honoring future."

—**Pam and Bill Farrel**, directors of Love-Wise, authors of *7 Simple skills for Every Woman, 7 Simple Skills for Every Man*, and best-selling *Men Are Like Waffles, Women Are Like Spaghetti*

"*Forsaken God?* equips us to intentionally remember the 'God-incidences' in our lives. Uniquely written, this book inspires us to embrace the profound significance of reflecting on our God-moments and to pass those memories on—and the faith strengthened by them—to the next generation. *Forsaken God?* is a powerful resource for individuals and small groups alike. I highly recommend it."

—**Stephani Shott**, founder of The MOM Initiative and author of *The Making of a Mom: Practical Help for Purposeful Parenting*

"*Forsaken God?* is a memory jogger that will explode your awareness of God's presence in this world and in your life. Filled with Scripture, true stories of God speaking into lives, and suggestions for remembering his goodness, Janet's latest book will encourage you to recognize God is alive and active. If you've ever questioned where God is, this book will help you find answers by discovering his presence in your own journey."

—**Poppy Smith**, MSFD, inspirational speaker, spiritual life coach, author of *I'm Too Young to Be This Old, I'm Too Human to Be Like Jesus, Reaching Higher,* and *Why Can't He Be More Like Me?*

FORSAKEN GOD?

FORSAKEN GOD?

REMEMBERING THE
GOODNESS OF GOD
OUR CULTURE HAS
FORGOTTEN

JANET THOMPSON

LEAFWOOD
PUBLISHERS
an imprint of Abilene Christian University Press

FORSAKEN GOD?

Remembering the Goodness of God Our Culture Has Forgotten

LEAFWOOD
P U B L I S H E R S
an imprint of Abilene Christian University Press

Copyright © 2016 by Janet Thompson

ISBN 978-0-89112-458-0

Printed in the United States of America

Cover design by ThinkPen Design, LLC

Interior text design by Sandy Armstrong, Strong Design

Leafwood Publishers is an imprint of Abilene Christian University Press
ACU Box 29138
Abilene, Texas 79699

1-877-816-4455
www.leafwoodpublishers.com

16 17 18 19 20 21 / 7 6 5 4 3 2 1

To Les and Pam Barnhart
for inspiring the vision for this book
and faithfully championing me.

Contents

Section Five—*Remembering God*

Acknowledgments

It's easy to remember God's goodness with the people he sends to help, encourage, pray for, and love me. *Forsaken God?* focuses on encouraging readers to faithfully remember God and challenges them to influence a world quickly forgetting God. The dark enemy of God worked his schemes to keep this book from seeing the light of day; but praise God, no weapon of the enemy could stop what God put into motion for his glory.

I will always remember and be grateful to the following:

- My Lord and Savior, you spurred me on with your Word and the Armor of God every morning as I prepared to go into battle with the enemy who tried to discourage and distract me. Look who's frustrated now. Praise God!
- My helpmate hubby Dave, you patiently tried to undo the enemy's efforts, prayed for me daily, and learned the fine art of heating up dinner for two—and sometimes one. I love you dearly and appreciate you unendingly.
- Les and Pam Barnhart, who helped birth the idea of this book. I love you both and thank God for our forever friendship.
- Dear friend Sharron Pankhurst, you eagerly ask with each new manuscript, "You're going to let me edit it, right?" Your detailed eyes are invaluable to every book I write. Thank you for serving me with your expertise and friendship.

- Becky Frye, for blessing us during manuscript deadlines with delicious homemade soups and sweet friendship. And Leanna and Bob Sforzini for bringing fabulous dinners, right to our doorstep.
- Pastor Brian Smith, your messages speak to whatever I'm writing about and Crouch Community Church prays for my speaking, writing, and traveling. I love our church!
- Nancy Matlack, who calls with encouraging Scriptures . . . I especially appreciate "Do not grow weary doing good."
- Our couples small group, who pray so faithfully for my ministry and life adventures.
- Walking buddy Gene Yundt, you traversed with me up and down our hill in snow, ice, rain, mud, and freezing temps, while patiently listening to the thousands of words I didn't get to verbalize while sequestered away writing.
- Sweet neighbor and friend Anita Sherwood, you understand my seclusion in my writing "tower" and consistently cheer me onward and upward.
- The men and women who shared stories, you were reminders of the many ways God is good to his people.
- My author–speaker colleagues who took time out of their busy schedules to write about how they remember God's goodness.
- Dr. David Stoop, your teaching inspired me at Fuller Theological Seminary—I will never forget the "relationship triangle." Thank you for your willingness to write the "Foreword" for a grateful student.
- Gary Meyers, you saw the potential for a book that could spur a revival of God's people if they will remember his goodness. It's a delight to do another book with Leafwood Publishers.

Foreword

When you first looked at the title for this book, you may have said to yourself something like, "Of course *I* would never forsake God. *I* always remember God's goodness, even if our culture has forgotten." But when trials and troubles hit, it's all too easy to forsake and forget. After all, the neuroscientists tell us we all have what's called a proclivity to the negative. Imagine you had twenty things happen to you during the day. Nineteen of them have been positive experiences and only one has been negative. But when you lay your head on your pillow at night, which of the things that happened to you will you focus on as you try to fall asleep? The negative one, of course. And what about our memories? We struggle to get rid of the negative, painful memories and struggle to remember the good.

That's why we need to develop strategies to help us remember the good things, especially the good things about God. God reminds us that we are to remember his actions. The Israelites were told to talk about God's goodness to their children. When something good happened, they built a pillar of stones so that later generations could ask, "What are those stones for?" And then they remembered what God had done at that place in times past.

God often takes the blame for most of our trials and troubles. We ask ourselves things like, "Why is God doing this to me?" But we don't give him the same credit when good things happen. It's like we all too often take credit for the good things, and blame God for the bad.

Janet Thompson has given us a much-needed resource for getting things in balance in our lives. She gives us the biblical basis for an aspect of God's character we are to remember, and then brings in personal stories of a number of people who illustrate that particular focus of their positive remembrances. But the real value in this book is in the suggestions in "Mentoring the Next Generation" and in the Appendix for ways we can train ourselves to focus on the positive rather than the negative, and remember the goodness of God.

David Stoop, PhD
clinical psychologist, ordained pastor, and
graduate and adjunct professor at Fuller Theological Seminary

Preface

I remain confident of this: I will see the goodness of the LORD in the land of the living.

—Psalm 27:13

"We have sinned with our fathers . . . [and] . . . did not remember . . ." (Psalm 106:6–7). Then prod your memory and wake up immediately. Don't say to yourself, "But God is not talking to me right now." He ought to be. Remember whose you are and whom you serve. Encourage yourself to remember, and your affection for God will increase tenfold. Your mind will no longer be starved, but will be quick and enthusiastic, and your help will be inexpressibly bright.

—Oswald Chambers[1]

Our nation is ridiculed abroad and morally crumbling within. We are in trouble. We have turned our back on God.

—Franklin Graham[2]

God put this book on my heart at 5:45 in the evening on May 31, 2006, while I was having dinner with dear friends Les and Pam Barnhart at Carrabba's Italian Grill in Nashville, Tennessee. I had salmon (my favorite food) and they split a chicken Italian pizza. How can I remember this occasion in such detail, and why is it important? Well, let me tell you the story.

I was on business in Nashville where the Barnharts lived then, so we went out to dinner together. At one time, Les had worked for me in Southern California when I managed an insurance agency, and since our families shared the same Christian faith, we developed a deep friendship, a kinship. We kept in touch over the years, so it was a delight to have quality catch-up time with this godly couple.

During dinner, our conversation turned into a discussion of how quickly we forget God's goodness when the next crisis arises. I pointed out how we readily criticize the Old Testament Israelites, who repeatedly forsook God and forgot his goodness, but aren't we the same today? We had just paid the bill and the receipt was lying on the table. As we discussed humanity's historical pattern of forgetting God's goodness, Les took the receipt, turned it over, and wrote on the back, "How Good is God? I Can't Remember . . ." Sliding the receipt across the table to me, he suggested, "This would be a great topic for a book!"

I took the receipt and put it in my purse for safekeeping. When I returned home, I started a folder labeled "How Good Is God? I Can't Remember . . ." and clipped the dinner receipt to the front of the folder. I added to my folder Scriptures, current events, and articles reflecting the theme of rejecting and forsaking God fueled by the forgetting of God's goodness, and then ways to remember his goodness. Over the years, the folder expanded with notes, Scriptures, and stories as I awaited God's timing to write this book. Several times seemed right, but God knew I needed more research and experiences to share with you. God's timing is always perfect—a vital aspect of his goodness to remember and never forget.

"How Good Is God? I Can't Remember . . ." evolved into the book you have in your hand—*Forsaken God?: Remembering the Goodness of God Our Culture Has Forgotten*. I don't expect that after reading *Forsaken God?* your mind will retain God-incidences with the same clarity and detail as I remember the origins of this book.

However, if you start saving important documents and mementos, writing in a prayer and praise journal, taking pictures, sharing your stories and testimony, and memorizing Scripture . . . you'll be well on your way to remembering God's goodness throughout your lifetime and passing memories on to the next generation. That's what I'm praying for you. That's what I think God meant at 5:45 in the evening on May 31, 2006, at Carrabba's Italian Grill in Nashville during a meaningful discussion with fellow believers! That's what I remember and will never forget, so . . .

I'll write the book on your righteousness,

talk up your salvation the livelong day,

never run out of good things to write or say.

I come in the power of the Lord God,

I post signs marking his right-of-way.

(Ps. 71:15–16 *The Message*)

Introduction

But watch out! Be careful never to forget what you yourself have seen. Do not let these memories escape from your mind as long as you live! And be sure to pass them on to your children and grandchildren.

—Deuteronomy 4:9 NLT

And I wish I could promise you, Elie [Holocaust survivor and Nobel Prize winner Elie Wiesel], that the lessons of history have been learned. I can only urge the leaders of the world not to repeat the mistakes of the past.

—Israeli Prime Minister Benjamin Netanyahu,
addressing the United States Congress, March 3, 2015

The most effective encouragement for trusting God in the *present* is remembering his power in the *past*.

When we forget someone's birthday or an important anniversary, we feel bad . . . but the forgotten person may grieve even more than we do, feeling unimportant, forsaken, or rejected. God grieves when we forget him: "How often they rebelled against him in the wilderness and grieved him in the wasteland! Again and again they put God to the test; they vexed the Holy One of Israel. They did not remember his power—the day he redeemed them from the oppressor" (Ps. 78:40–42).

We grieve losing anything we consider valuable. We mourn the loss of memorabilia or heirlooms, a family pet, the perfect job, a loved one. But do we mourn as intensely the loss of our memory of God's hand in our life . . . in the life of our family . . . in the life of our nation? You don't get over grief by forgetting—you get through grief by remembering.

Our memories validate and preserve the significance of people, events, circumstances, and accomplishments. When we forget about them, their relevance diminishes. We live in a culture quickly forgetting the goodness of God and, thus, the relevance of God. God knew there would be a propensity to forget him and the wonders he has done, so throughout the Bible he reminds believers never to forget him or his goodness and warns of subsequent destruction through all generations to those who don't take this warning seriously. In *Forsaken God?*, we'll look at many biblical references for remembering God because Scripture, the foundation of our faith, is the same yesterday, today, and tomorrow, and it applies to *every* generation, era, and culture. Here are just a few reminders:

- Remember well what the LORD your God did to Pharaoh and to all Egypt (Deut. 7:18).
- Remember the Lord, who is great and awesome, and fight for your families, your sons and your daughters, your wives and your homes (Neh. 4:14b).
- Remember the former things, those of long ago; I am God, and there is no other; I am God, and there is none like me (Isa. 46:9).
- Do you have eyes but fail to see, and ears but fail to hear? And don't you remember? (Mark 8:18).
- Remember Lot's wife! Whoever tries to keep their life will lose it, and whoever loses their life will preserve it (Luke 17:32–33).

- Remember that for three years I never stopped warning each of you night and day with tears (Acts 20:31).

God, and his God-inspired writers, stressed the importance of creating a culture of memories. If we don't remember what God already has done, we won't believe what he is capable of doing in the future. Memory builds faith.

Memories preserve the mighty works of God, but how many godly men and women failed to write down, or tell of, the miracles they saw God perform? How many works, deeds, and miracles has God done in your life . . . in my life . . . in the lives of our families . . . that we took for granted and never shared or acknowledged? These miraculous acts of faith are lost to the next generation and lost to us when we need most to remember God's goodness to help us through a trial or tribulation.

Today, society marginalizes, neutralizes, and denies God—he's forgotten by a culture forsaking him. It's time for Christians to step up, speak out, and seize opportunities to defend God—as Franklin Graham warns—"before we lose our country!" Exerting boldness for God requires drawing from our own memories of God's goodness—sharing with a disparaging world the greatness of our God and the things we've seen him do. We'll be swimming upstream in a sinking culture, but some will reach out to Jesus for the salvation life preserver and will survive.

Even the most dedicated believers have times when they forget God. Most don't intentionally forget God; they just don't try hard enough to remember him. The challenges of living in today's world ensnare everyone's focus and attention. Multiple situations vie simultaneously for our attention and memory: immediate demands, emergencies, needs, wants, activities, experiences, lifestyle, work, parenting, family. The list goes on.

Intentionally remembering God's goodness begins when we answer this question: Is God good? Most believers would answer,

"Of course God is good." Then we need to act like we believe it. Believing God is good + following his instructions = a good life. Isn't that what we all want for our families and ourselves? Then let's start shouting about his goodness from the rooftops: "One generation commends your works to another; they tell of your mighty acts" (Ps. 145:4).

It only takes one generation forgetting the goodness of God to erase God completely from our culture. That should challenge us, scare us a little, and hopefully motivate us a lot to put God where he belongs—*first* in our families, *first* in our minds, *first* in our days, *first* in our lives, *first* in our nation. It will be hard to forget him when he's *first* in everything we think, do, and say.

Today's culture wants to silence any mention of God or Jesus. Our forefathers in the faith and in our nation would be aghast at a twenty-first century culture where invoking the name of God or Jesus, or saying you're a Christian, could possibly get you fined, expelled from school, fired, sued, incarcerated, or even executed. Yet people around the world still acknowledge the memory and existence of Jesus every time they say or write the date—the number of days since Christ walked the earth. Sadly, the general populace doesn't know, or has forgotten, the significance and origin of today's date.

Retailers and focus groups rally to take Christ out of Christmas and outlaw manger scenes, crosses, and religious symbols in the public square. They've forgotten, or discount, that the sole purpose of Christmas is to celebrate Christ's birth. And we celebrate Easter because Christ died on the cross to atone for our sins and rose three days later to offer every person who believes in him eternal life. How many people understand or honor these truths today? How many Christians fail to teach these truths in their families, from generation to generation? How many Christians are going with the flow and allowing the silencing of truth while watching the moral foundation of our country collapse?

Francis Chan, in his book *Forgotten God*, challenges born-again Christians: "Yet when those outside the church see no difference in our lives, they begin to question our integrity, our sanity, or even worse, our God. And can you blame them?"[1] We all need a memory jogger of God's relevance in our world . . . our families . . . our churches . . . our communities . . . and our own lives. And we need our actions and lifestyle to reflect the morals and values of the Jesus we follow.

Sometimes remembering rehearses difficult seasons we would rather forget; but remembering also helps us to acknowledge God's significant role in the incident. There are times when "holy forgetting" is appropriate—our past sins, mistakes, shame, or guilt. We don't let these things define us. Once we ask Jesus to come into our hearts and lives and ask forgiveness for our past transgressions and sins, he wipes the slate clean, and the Bible tells us he remembers them no more . . . neither should we with a sense of shame or guilt. But we should never forget the pit we were in when Jesus held out his hand to pull us up out of the mire and how only his redeeming grace saved us. We remember where we came from so we never return to or repeat where we've been.

"Holy remembering" captures our past in the light of God's powerful, wise, and always-good presence in the life of every believer. Remembering our faults brings despair; remembering God's faithfulness brings joy. Can you imagine the revival if Christians actively influenced the culture to remember God? My challenge to you is together let's start a bold and brave movement to create a God-centered culture that remembers the magnificent goodness of our great God in our homes, communities, and churches.

Revival starts with impassioned faith. Faith believes in what we don't see now. Faith's reward is seeing what we believe come true and then acknowledging that the miracle we just experienced is really from God. Remember the story of Jesus instructing the disciples to feed the five thousand in Mark 6:30–44, and how there was enough to feed everyone with twelve baskets left over? Yet when the next crowd of four thousand gathered (Mark 8:1–9), the disciples again lacked faith and lamented there was nothing to feed the people, even though they had seven loaves of bread and had recently watched Jesus feed five thousand people with only five loaves of bread. How could they forget such a miracle so quickly?

Jesus asked them the same question when they went out to sea in a boat after feeding the four thousand with seven loaves of bread, and yet they were again worrying because there was no bread with them in the boat.

> The disciples had forgotten to bring bread, except for one loaf they had with them in the boat. "Be careful," Jesus warned them. "Watch out for the yeast of the Pharisees and that of Herod."
>
> They discussed this with one another and said, "It is because we have no bread."
>
> Aware of their discussion, Jesus asked them: "Why are you talking about having no bread? Do you still not see or understand? Are your hearts hardened? Do you have eyes but fail to see, and ears but fail to hear? And don't you remember? When I broke the five loaves for the five thousand, how many basketfuls of pieces did you pick up?"
>
> "Twelve," they replied.
>
> "And when I broke the seven loaves for the four thousand, how many basketfuls of pieces did you pick up?"
>
> They answered, "Seven."
>
> He said to them, "Do you still not understand?"
> (Mark 8:14–21)

Just like the disciples, every Christian sees God doing miracles in his or her life . . . becoming a Christian is a miracle in itself. Still,

God asks us the same question Jesus asked the disciples, "Do you still not understand?"

It would be catastrophic bedlam if God, the Creator of the world, remembered us only as often as we remember him. In *Crazy Love*, Francis Chan asks the question we should all ask ourselves: "Why are we so quick to forget God? Who do we think we are? I find myself relearning this lesson often. Even though I glimpse God's holiness, I am still dumb enough to forget that life is all about God and not about me at all."[2] Spiritual amnesia ensues when we take credit for our accomplishments and forget God's goodness. Spiritual remembering ensues when we humbly give God the glory for the things he has done. It's the age-old tug-of-war between pride and humility, and the Bible says God hates one and loves the other (James 4:6).

The good news is there's hope for us, just like there was for the disciples. After Jesus died and rose again three days later and walked among them, they finally got it: "After he was raised from the dead, his disciples recalled what he had said. Then they believed the scripture and the words that Jesus had spoken" (John 2:22). The disciples started remembering all Jesus had done right before their eyes—casting out demons, healing the sick, raising Lazarus from the dead, causing the lame to walk and the blind to see, turning water into wine. They remembered the biggest miracle of all, the gospel message. Jesus had predicted that he would die on a cross and arise again in three days to offer eternal life to his followers: "At first his disciples did not understand all this. Only after Jesus was glorified did they realize that these things had been written about him and that these things had been done to him" (John 12:16).

Praise God . . . Matthew, Mark, Luke, and John wrote down all they remembered of their time with Jesus, and we have access to their memories through the first four books in the New Testament, the Gospels. Luke and John, along with the apostle Paul and several of Jesus's brothers, wrote the balance of the New Testament. Old

Testament prophets and men of God recorded all they saw God do and what he inspired them to write. Thanks to these saints answering God's call, we have a book of God's goodness—the Bible—so we should *never* forget or forsake our God, his Son Jesus Christ, and the Holy Spirit. We know with conviction and authority that *every* word in the Bible is God-breathed (2 Tim. 3:16).

Forsaken God? is teeming with memory-jogging Scripture, because I don't have any new and unique insight God hasn't said already in his Word. The Bible is the basis for our faith, not my words. My prayer is that I'll spark your interest to search out and discover the value of using God's Word to remember how good he has been to you, and to use your Bible as a guide to traverse the world's minefield God allows Satan to rule until Jesus returns.

Satan won't like you making a concerted effort to remember God. Satan wants you to forget God's goodness. Let that sink in a minute. If you forget God and his role in your life, then Satan has you just where he wants you. Satan's target is believers. He doesn't care about those who love the world because he already has them in his grip. He focuses on luring believers to love something else more than they love God. Satan wants to break God's heart. Unfortunately, he seems to be succeeding in many areas. If he can get believers to look to the world's ways and forget God's ways, Satan smirks.

It's imperative for Christians to know Scripture because God's Word is the sword of the Spirit—the only offensive weapon you have against the enemy—Satan. If you're not reading your Bible and don't know what God says about how to live the Christian life, you'll become a casualty of the spiritual war. I don't want that fate for you and I know you don't either; but I do want you aware that Satan will do whatever he can to prevent you from reading *Forsaken God?*—*especially* the Ways to Remember God's Goodness prompts. The good news is you can daily prepare for this battle by putting on the armor of God found in Ephesians 6:10–18. I don't start my day without praying this:

> Finally, be strong in the Lord and in his mighty power. Put on the full armor of God, so that you can take your stand against the devil's schemes. For our struggle is not against flesh and blood, but against the rulers, against the authorities, against the powers of this dark world and against the spiritual forces of evil in the heavenly realms. Therefore put on the full armor of God, so that when the day of evil comes, you may be able to stand your ground, and after you have done everything, to stand. Stand firm then, with the belt of truth buckled around your waist, with the breastplate of righteousness in place, and with your feet fitted with the readiness that comes from the gospel of peace. In addition to all this, take up the shield of faith, with which you can extinguish all the flaming arrows of the evil one. Take the helmet of salvation and the sword of the Spirit, which is the word of God. And pray in the Spirit on all occasions with all kinds of prayers and requests. With this in mind, be alert and always keep on praying for all the Lord's people.

Okay, you're suited up in your spiritual armor. Now let's delve into ways to remember God so that you can leave the legacy of a life that professed and enjoyed the goodness of God.

Book Design

In *Forsaken God?* each chapter begins with "Bible Memories," where we look at passages of Scripture and biblical stories for examples of God's Word on a particular topic. You might want your Bible near as you read.

Next, godly men and women contribute vulnerable personal stories of how they forgot God's goodness and ways that help them to "Remember God's Goodness." When I sent out a call for stories, it was a blessing to have so many friends and fellow authors and speakers (names included in stories) willing to share the goodness they have witnessed God perform in their lives.

In "My Memories," I share times I forgot the wonders and miracles of God and, subsequently, the ways I found to help me remember.

Then I give you an opportunity to recall "Your Memories" and suggest specific "Ways to Remember God's Goodness." There is space for you to record your thoughts so you can revisit them later as a memory refresher.

"Let's Pray" is a prayer for you to personalize in asking God to help you remember the specific "goodness" characteristic of God discussed in the chapter.

"Talk about It" includes questions and conversation starters for discussion in small groups, Bible study groups, book clubs, or with family and friends. Discussing with others what we read is a proven way to enhance memory. If you're reading this book on your own, still answer the questions as another way to engage with and remember the content of the chapter.

I pray you will share the passion God has impressed upon me for Christians to maintain vivid memories of God's goodness and keep those memories in the forefront of our hearts, minds, and souls. My heart's desire is for you to share those memories with your families, your sphere of influence, and a lost world.

SECTION
ONE

RECOGNIZING
GOD

God's wisdom is so deep, God's power so immense, who could take him on and come out in one piece? He moves mountains before they know what's happened, flips them on their heads on a whim. He gives the earth a good shaking up, rocks it down to its very foundations. He tells the sun, "Don't shine," and it doesn't; he pulls the blinds on the stars. All by himself he stretches out the heavens and strides on the waves of the sea. He designed the Big Dipper and Orion, the Pleiades and Alpha Centauri. We'll never comprehend all the great things he does; his miracle-surprises can't be counted. Somehow, though he moves right in front of me, I don't see him; quietly but surely he's active, and I miss it.

—Job 9:4–11 *The Message*

When my Presence is the focal point of your consciousness,
all the pieces of your life fall into place.

—Sarah Young[1]

Recognizing God is a prerequisite to *experiencing* his goodness and *remembering* what he has done in our lives.

The word *recognize* has several meanings depending on its use and context.

- **Formal acknowledgment:** I recognize God as Lord and sovereign.
- **Recall from memory:** I recognize God in this situation because I remember him doing the same thing in the past.
- **Verifying a truth:** I recognize God's Word is infallible.
- **In agreement with:** I recognize the Bible as my guide for life.
- **Worthy of being heard:** I recognize and give my attention to God's voice.
- **Encountered before (re—again, cognize—to know):** I recognize God because I know him.

As Job expressed in the opening passage, often God moves right in front of us and we miss him because we aren't looking for him in our ordinary, daily activities. We may relegate God's accomplishments solely to performing miracles or answering prayer requests—only noticing him when his actions are spectacular—or attributing those actions to fate or serendipity.

Perhaps we expect God to perform the same way every time or don't recognize a miracle when we see it—a baby's birth, the human body, the seasons, the solar system—everyday miracles of God.

We miss God in the sound of a bird chirping—forgetting he created birds, each with distinct sounds. We expect grass to grow—minimizing God's handiwork. We enjoy refreshing rain—ignoring that it's a blessing from God's sky. We know the sun will rise every morning and the moon at night. I wonder about those who don't believe in God: Who do they think makes that happen *every* day and night, without fail?

God is *everywhere* and in *everything*, but do we stop and give him the glory *every time*?

Chapter One

Recognizing His Voice

When he has brought out all his own, he goes on ahead of them, and his sheep follow him because they know his voice. But they will never follow a stranger; in fact, they will run away from him because they do not recognize a stranger's voice.

—John 10:4–5

I find that when I pay attention to God and what he's asking of me, he richly rewards me. And when I ignore his voice (pretend I can't hear it clearly), I face a life lesson, usually a painful one. So why is it so difficult to obey the voice of God?

—Heidi Williams

Bible Memories

The Israelites saw God's amazing miracles as he freed them from slavery with the ten plagues, parted the Red Sea, and then guided them in a cloud by day and fire by night, but they forgot God's goodness. God gave them daily provision of food and water, they heard his voice (Deut. 4:36), and he spoke to them "face to face" out of a fire (Deut. 5:4); still, they repeatedly forgot.

During their years of captivity in Egypt, the Israelites couldn't hear God through their complaining and pain: "'And I will bring you to the land I swore with uplifted hand to give to Abraham, to

Isaac and to Jacob. I will give it to you as a possession. I am the LORD.' Moses reported this to the Israelites, but they did not listen to him because of their discouragement and harsh labor" (Exod. 6:8–9). But even after their miraculous fleeing and freeing from slavery, they were infamous for recognizing God's provision in the moment, but quickly forgetting his past goodness when the next need or want arose.

After crossing the Red Sea, they traveled for three days in the desert without water, and when they did find water it was bitter, and so were they. God heard their grumbling and made the water sweet by having Moses throw a piece of wood into the water. But God spoke an ultimatum:

> There the LORD issued a ruling and instruction for them and put them to the test. He said, "If you *listen carefully to the voice of the LORD your God* and do what is right in his eyes, if you pay attention to his commands and keep all his decrees, I will not bring on you any of the diseases I brought on the Egyptians, for I am the LORD, who heals you." Then they came to Elim, where there were twelve springs and seventy palm trees, and they camped there near the water. (Exod. 15:25b–27 NIV 1984; emphasis added)

Next, they wanted food, so the Lord rained down manna, "bread from heaven," and quail when they demanded meat. Then he commanded them to start moving, but again there was no water and again they complained.

> They said, "Why did you bring us up out of Egypt to make us and our children and livestock die of thirst?"
>
> Then Moses cried out to the LORD, "What am I to do with these people? They are almost ready to stone me."

The LORD answered Moses, "Go out in front of the people. Take with you some of the elders of Israel and take in your hand the staff with which you struck the Nile, and go. I will stand there before you by the rock at Horeb. Strike the rock, and water will come out of it for the people to drink." So Moses did this in the sight of the elders of Israel. And he called the place Massah and Meribah because the Israelites quarreled and because they tested the LORD saying, "Is the LORD among us or not?" (Exod. 17:3b–7)

Is the Lord among us or not? Don't we still ask this today? Like the Israelites, we've seen God do amazing things in our lives, and we've heard his voice, but the next time we're in need, we test him again and doubt he'll come through for us. We never saw the Israelites stop to pray and ask God in faith for help. Instead, they quarreled with Moses, their mediator between them and God and their leader who had faced Pharaoh and helped them flee oppression. They forgot how good God had been at orchestrating their freedom from bondage. They took God and Moses for granted—only as good as the next miracle or provision. So the Lord purposely let the people hear his voice:

The LORD said to Moses, "I am going to come to you in a dense cloud, so that the people will hear me speaking with you and will always put their trust in you." Then Moses told the LORD what the people had said. And the LORD said to Moses, "Go to the people and consecrate them today and tomorrow. Have them wash their clothes and be ready by the third day, because on that day the LORD will come down on Mount Sinai in the sight of all the people. (Exod. 19:9–11)

Then Moses went to the top of Mount Sinai to meet with God, who *spoke* the Ten Commandments while the people waited at the bottom of the mountain (Exod. 20:1). But while Moses was with the Lord, the people forgot they had been in the presence of Almighty God and had heard his voice. The Lord said to Moses, "How quickly they have turned away from the way I commanded them to live! They have melted down gold and made a calf, and they have bowed down and sacrificed to it. They are saying, 'These are your gods, O Israel, who brought you out of the land of Egypt'" (Exod. 32:8 NLT).

Moses talked God out of annihilating the people, but the Israelites' continual forgetfulness and ungratefulness caused the first generation freed from Egypt to miss the biggest blessing of all—the Promised Land. Forgetting all the good God had done for them in their freedom journey out of Egypt, they rejected God's gift of the land flowing with milk and honey, for fear of the "giants" living there. Moses tried to reason with them, but they wouldn't listen. So God appeared to them again and spoke in a voice they had to acknowledge:

> But the whole assembly talked about stoning [Moses and Aaron]. Then the glory of the LORD appeared at the Tent of Meeting to all the Israelites. The LORD said to Moses, "How long will these people treat me with contempt? How long will they refuse to believe in me, in spite of all the miraculous signs I have performed among them? I will strike them down with a plague and destroy them, but I will make you into a nation greater and stronger than they." (Num. 14:10–12 NIV 1984)

Again, Moses talked God out of killing these stubborn, rebellious people, but there was a consequence of forgetting God's goodness to them:

The LORD replied, "I have forgiven them, as you asked. Nevertheless, as surely as I live and as surely as the glory of the LORD fills the whole earth, not one of those who saw my glory and the those signs I performed in Egypt and in the wilderness but who disobeyed me and tested me ten times—not one of them will ever see the land I promised on oath to their ancestors. No one who has treated me with contempt will ever see it." (Num. 14:20–23)

Sadly, even Moses forgot God's goodness in giving precise instructions to sustain their lives, and this forgetfulness prevented him also from entering the Promised Land. After seeing and hearing God in a burning bush and watching him inscribe the Ten Commandments on stone, how could Moses forget to listen carefully to God's voice? Moses's downfall evolved from trying to please a group of people who routinely forgot God's goodness.

The LORD said to Moses, "Take the staff, and you and your brother Aaron gather the assembly together. Speak to that rock before their eyes and it will pour out its water. You will bring water out of the rock for the community so they and their livestock can drink."

So Moses took the staff from the LORD's presence, just as he commanded him. He and Aaron gathered the assembly together in front of the rock and Moses said to them, "Listen, you rebels, must we bring you water out of this rock?" Then Moses raised his arm and struck the rock twice with his staff. Water gushed out, and the community and their livestock drank.

But the LORD said to Moses and Aaron, "Because you did not trust in me enough to honor me as holy in the sight of the Israelites, you will not bring this community into the land I give them." (Num. 20:7–12)

God wanted Moses to *speak* the water from the rock—an even more miraculous witness to God's power than when Moses previously *hit* the rock for water. Moses acted the way God said *last* time rather than listening carefully to God's voice *this* time. That can happen to us, too, when we let our emotions or the voices of others drown out the powerful voice of God speaking to us today—the same voice that *spoke* Creation into being in the beginning.

Debbie Remembers God's Goodness

My dear friend Debbie relates to the forgetfulness of the Israelites and Moses. She was studying the above passages in Bible Study Fellowship (BSF), when she recognized God's voice warning her she too was guilty of forgetting God's goodness and provision.

My husband and I are in real estate and we finally closed a transaction we'd been working on for months. Realtors don't receive payment until the transaction closes. We were both very excited and thankful to God for his provision.

But two days after the closing, as I was driving up our street, I noticed a new "For Sale" sign on a home owned by a nice Christian family we have known for some time; but they had listed with another realtor. Extremely disappointed, I wondered how God could let this happen. Why didn't we get the listing? I moped and was depressed for the rest of the day.

Finally, by the end of my self-made miserable day, I remembered our BSF study from last week. God had repeatedly provided for the Israelites and they chose not to remember his previous provision and instead grumbled about their lack of current provision. Instantly, I recognized God reminding me I was behaving exactly like the Israelites!

I immediately repented, asking God's forgiveness for my lack of appreciation of his provision and lack of trust that he will continue providing for our needs. The moping and depression lifted and God filled me with joy for how faithful he is to us. I pray that in the future, I will not disappoint God by forgetting his faithfulness to us in the past. Thank you, Lord!

My Memories

In January 1993, after rededicating my life to God the previous year, I felt a nudge from the Holy Spirit to study his Word in depth. I asked the Lord, "Where do you want me to go to learn more about you?" *Seminary.*

"School?" After receiving an MBA, I remember saying, "I'll never go to school again!" Just to humor God, I decided to research a couple of seminary programs in the area.

When all the brochures arrived, I decided the seminaries were too expensive and too far away. The year passed with no further action on my part to pursue seminary, until one day a large envelope arrived in the mail with a return address from Fuller Theological Seminary. I hadn't requested information from Fuller Seminary.

I opened the envelope and pulled out the cover letter addressed to me and welcoming me to the Winter Quarter at Fuller's Orange County Extension program—I lived in Orange County! No one at Fuller could explain why I received the packet. Divine intervention does get your attention. How can you ignore it? I didn't. I recognized God's voice: *Will you step out in faith and trust me, even if you don't know now where I am leading you?*

One year into seminary, I began wondering what God's plans were for me, since I'd said I would serve him in any area *except* women's ministry. Seeking direction, I attended a Women in Ministry Leadership Conference in Portland, Oregon. The second day of the conference, April 25, 1995, I again heard God's voice calling me. This time, he said—*Go feed my sheep.* I asked, "What sheep? Where? And what would I feed them if I found them?" I just heard again: *Feed my sheep.*

I said an obedient "okay" and wondered whom I was talking to and what I had just agreed to do. I prayed about it on the phone that night with my husband, and he prayed the Holy Spirit would reveal the meaning of "feed my sheep."

God answered our prayer and confirmed his call for me when the next morning the training was from John 21:15–17, where Jesus tells Peter, "Feed my sheep." The title of the workshop was Shepherding Women in Your Church. "Oh no, Lord! Remember I don't want to work with women." But I had clearly heard the Lord's voice, and I had agreed to do whatever he asked.

Your Memories

A. W. Tozer advised, "God is not silent. It is the nature of God to speak. The Voice of God is a friendly Voice. No one need fear to listen to it unless he has already made up his mind to resist it."[1]

Everyone's journey is different, and the Lord reveals himself to each person in a unique way—one he or she will recognize. He calls in a voice he knows will speak best to *you*—be ready, listening, and willing. He'll often speak in the ordinary circumstances of your day. The challenge is to stop long enough to hear his voice—to listen. As you become responsive to his subtle messages, he'll move on to the more obvious—the ones that seem to light up in neon.

You might be wondering how God speaks and how you can know it's him. The first step is to believe in Jesus and accept him into your heart so the Holy Spirit dwells in you. If you've taken that step, you heard God in your spirit and soul and acknowledged his voice by answering and accepting him as your Lord and Savior.

Now you need to get into his Word, the Bible, and read it voraciously because he speaks to all of us through the Scriptures, just as he did to Debbie and to me.

If you haven't accepted Jesus as your Lord and Savior but would like to now, go to page 264 in the Appendix and pray A Salvation Prayer. Then begin reading your Bible, listening, and looking for God at work in your life.

My readers often say, "I heard your voice in your writing." Authors learn to write in their own voice and not try to sound like someone else. God speaks in *his* voice through his written Word: the Holy Bible.

God also speaks to us through fellow believers, pastors, sermons, songs, books, speakers, circumstances, prayer . . . even some movies. He's always talking to believers, just as he did to the Israelites, but they often choose to ignore, or forget, what they hear him say. Spiritual discernment (determining truth from error according to God's Word) and prayer (talking to God) will help you recognize how God speaks to you today.

Debbie and I both recognized God speaking to us to get our attention. Where have you recognized God's voice? Remember a God-encounter in your past. Now think back to the various ways God spoke to you during this incident and list those here.

God told me that my situation was "between Him & I" — He told me "to just wait a little longer" & he revealed the answer I was seeking for someone I loved.

Ways to Remember God's Goodness—
A Daily Quiet Time

The noise of the world can drown out the distinctive voice of God—"Be still, and know that I am God" (Ps. 46:10). There's no better way to hear the Lord than finding a quiet place alone—just

God and you. It might be in your home, yard, office, car . . . find a special spot and time where you can read your Bible, pray, and hear God *every day*. You may only have a few minutes, but God will be waiting for you there.

Put this daily date with God on your calendar and schedule the rest of your life around it. If you don't make time with God a priority, other things will eat up your day. You may have to get up a little earlier in the morning or eliminate something from your schedule, but it will be well worth it. When considering what to eliminate, look for something that *doesn't* have kingdom value.

If you're going through a tough time, God's trying to talk to you, but maybe you're not hearing him because the sounds of turmoil are outshouting the still, small voice of the Lord. During those times—we all have them—stealing away with the Lord will reassure you God hasn't gone anywhere. He's still waiting for you to come and sit with him for a while.

Make a practice throughout the day of listening for God and noticing *when* and *how* he speaks to you. Is it through the Bible, a pastor, a song, a book, a blog, a person, a TV show or movie, the radio, or something else? Jot down these moments and the venue God used so you can remember the various ways God has of speaking into *your* heart.

Always date what you write. Did you notice in My Memories I knew the exact day God called me into ministry when I heard, "Feed my sheep"? You never want to forget significant moments in your life, so mark them on your calendar.

Let's Pray

Lord, please help me recognize your voice. Give me ears to hear and eyes to see your wonders, wisdom, power, and love for me. I want to choose to remember your good deeds and not my own faults and failures. I know I can do this with the strength that comes from knowing your Son, Jesus Christ. Amen.

Talk about It

1. Remember a time when God spoke to you through Scripture. Did you recognize his voice and did you obey? Why or why not?

He used "a gentle answer turns away wrath."
Yes, I obeyed & it affected the outcome positively

2. Discuss the following verse in reference to recognizing, hearing, and remembering God.

> Seek the LORD and His strength; seek His face evermore! Remember His marvelous works which He has done, His wonders, and the judgments of His mouth." (Ps. 105:4–5 NKJV)

3. How did God speak to Elijah in the following passage? How does he speak to you?

> The LORD said, "Go out and stand on the mountain in the presence of the LORD, for the LORD is about to pass by." Then a great and powerful wind tore the mountains apart and shattered the rocks before the LORD, but the LORD was not in the wind. After the wind there was an earthquake, but the LORD was not in the earthquake. After the earthquake came a fire, but the LORD was

not in the fire. And after the fire came a gentle whisper. When Elijah heard it, he pulled his cloak over his face and went out and stood at the mouth of the cave. (1 Kings 19:11–13)

4. Discuss ways to hear God's voice.

- Prayer
- God's Word reveals His voice to me
- messages or radio
- Christian radio

God thank you that you are speaking to me always, speaking me your truth, help me to be listening, aware of your speaking.

Chapter Two

Recognizing His Presence

All of you are standing today in the presence of the LORD your God.
—Deuteronomy 29:10a

*Let your mind linger on the ways God has revealed
His presence to you.*
—Poppy Smith[1]

Bible Memories

Moses had the honor of being in God's presence. Even though Moses never saw a form, he saw God in a burning bush, a fog, a cloud, and "thick darkness" (Exod. 20:21), and he heard God's voice. The Israelites also saw God's presence leading them through the wilderness by a cloud during the day and fire by night (Exod. 13:21), or when he covered the top of Mount Sinai with a thick cloud and smoke and spoke to them (Exod. 19:16–19). They knew it was God.

Moses admonishes the new generation, who are soon to possess the land God promised, never to forget the times they and their forefathers heard God's voice and were in his presence:

> Only be careful, and watch yourselves closely so that you do not forget the things your eyes have seen or let them fade from your heart as long as you live. Teach

them to your children and to their children after them. Remember the day you stood before the LORD your God at Horeb, when he said to me, "Assemble the people before me to hear my words so that they may learn to revere me as long as they live in the land and may teach them to their children." You came near and stood at the foot of the mountain while it blazed with fire to the very heavens, with black clouds and deep darkness. Then the LORD spoke to you out of the fire. You heard the sound of words but saw no form; there was only a voice. He declared to you his covenant, the Ten Commandments, which he commanded you to follow and then wrote them on two stone tablets. And the LORD directed me at that time to teach you the decrees and laws you are to follow in the land that you are crossing the Jordan to possess. (Deut. 4:9–14)

Moses then warned the people that even though they had not seen God in physical body, everywhere they look they see his presence in creation. The sky, sun, moon, stars, animals, birds, fish are all reminders God is with us *every* moment—a constant reflection of his goodness and presence. However, only God the Creator deserves worship, not his creation (Deut. 4:15–20).

Next, Moses reminds them that because *he* forgot God's goodness and didn't acknowledge God's voice and presence, only *one* time, he wouldn't be leading them into the Promised Land. He warns them again: "Be careful not to forget the covenant of the LORD your God that he made with you; do not make for yourselves an idol in the form of anything the LORD your God has forbidden. For the LORD your God is a consuming fire, a jealous God" (Deut. 4:23–24).

Moses implores them to acknowledge how incomparably good God is and to obey God's commands so it might be well with them and future generations:

Ask now about the former days, long before your time, from the day God created human beings on the earth; ask from one end of the heavens to the other. Has anything so great as this ever happened, or has anything like it ever been heard of? Has any other people heard the voice of God speaking out of fire, as you have, and lived? Has any god ever tried to take for himself one nation out of another nation, by testings, by signs and wonders, by war, by a mighty hand and an outstretched arm, or by great and awesome deeds, like all the things the LORD your God did for you in Egypt before your very eyes?

You were shown these things so that you might know that the LORD is God; besides him there is no other. From heaven he made you hear his voice to discipline you. On earth he showed you his great fire, and you heard his words from out of the fire. Because he loved your ancestors and chose their descendants after them, he brought you out of Egypt by his Presence and his great strength, to drive out before you nations greater and stronger than you and to bring you into their land to give it to you for your inheritance, as it is today.

Acknowledge and take to heart this day that the LORD is God in heaven above and on the earth below. There is no other. Keep his decrees and commands, which I am giving you today, so that it may go well with you and your children after you and that you may live long in the land the LORD your God gives you for all time. (Deut. 4:32–40)

The people recognized that they heard God's voice and experienced his presence, so they promised Moses they would obey God: "Go near and listen to all that the LORD our God says. Then tell us whatever the LORD our God tells you. We will listen and obey" (Deut. 5:27). But they quickly forgot and disobeyed, and there would be consequences: "You who were as numerous as the stars in the sky will be left but few in number, because you did not obey the LORD your God" (Deut. 28:62).

The Israelites saw God's presence in memorable ways, yet they still didn't recognize his goodness and greatness. God shows his presence in memorable ways to us, too, but how well do we recognize him? We're *always* in his presence. "The LORD is with you when you are with him. If you seek him, he will be found by you, but if you forsake him, he will forsake you" (2 Chron. 15:2b).

We forsake him and do the walking away when we become indifferent to the splendid goodness we see him doing in the world around us. The beauty of creation is a constant reminder of his presence, but we can become complacent and ho-hum about the sun rising every morning and the moon and stars illuminating every night—rivers and oceans halting at the shore, majestic mountains, beautiful plains, and breathtaking deserts. God envelops us in daily visual reminders of his presence, but familiarity often breeds apathy.

Raini Bowles Remembers God's Goodness

Raini will never forget how good God was in starting her ministry, SHINE ON, because she *heard* God's voice, *recognized* his presence, and obeyed.

I have no idea what I'm doing and no one to walk me through it. Everything has been by trial and error and God's leading.

My initial idea for a women's group was a Women's Potluck Fellowship, with meetings held in the park—not always comfortable or weather conducive. Next, I tried a diner, but it's difficult to praise the Lord or speak openly in that setting. When we finally met in someone's house, seventeen women attended from seven area churches.

Reluctantly, I had to take a break in the winter, but I prayed about the future of this group—on my heart for so long. Several months later, in the wee hours of the morning, I got up with an acronym in my mind— SHINE—Share, Help, Inspire, Nurture, and Encourage. I loved it!

I began searching the Internet for a suitable website name. *Aplacetoshine.org* was open, and as I clicked on it, "Congratulations!" popped up on my screen. Apparently, I had a domain credit and was suddenly the shocked owner of aplacetoshine.org.

I took the website as a sign from God and began working on a place to hold SHINE ON, but I hit a wall. So I prayed until one day I clearly heard: *Why would I give you a place when you have done nothing to fill it?* Ouch!

I understood and struggled with the thought that God was asking me to step out in faith *now* and find someone to speak and someone to lead worship. I called the first person on my speakers list to ask if she would pray about speaking; but she said, "I've already prayed, and the answer is yes." I was dazed!

So I had a speaker and a date . . . gulp . . . but no location. I would've panicked had I not known I was following God's direction.

A recurring thought lingered—a long shot and an odd location. I had been an office administrator at a doctor's office, and it would be a great place for SHINE ON . . . unusual . . . but perfect. When I called the doctor to ask if I could hold a monthly group event in his building, I received a resounding yes. Once again, my jaw hit the floor. I know God is capable and I have faith he will do things beyond my imagination, but when it *really* happens . . . it's humbling and astonishing.

I now had a place, a date, and a speaker . . . all I needed was women. I put the word out again. Even if he chose only one woman to attend and we helped her, or she became a believer, it would be worth it.

Nine women from six different churches attended the first meeting. God showed up and did amazing things. I had a plan for SHINE ON, but God's plan was better—not clean and smooth—but perfect for his purpose. SHINE ON is all about God. I'm doing this because I recognize God's call and his presence in my life.

My Memories

Several weeks after attending the Women in Ministry Conference where I heard God's call to "feed my sheep," my little flock began taking shape. God presented a series of events revealing that *feeding* meant mentoring and the *sheep* were definitely women.

- A woman in my business asked me to mentor her.
- My stepdaughter's small group asked me to be a group mentor.
- A college woman visiting the small group said her summer assignment was to find a mentor and asked me to mentor her.
- I saw the young adults' pastor at Saddleback Church working out at the gym and told him my "feed my sheep"

story. We never saw each other at the gym before or after that day, even though I went daily.

- The young adults' pastor introduced me to the pastor to new ministries, and they both felt God was calling me to start a women's mentoring ministry at Saddleback Church.

- The pastor to new ministries handed me the 12 Planning Steps for Developing a Ministry at Saddleback, and with the encouragement of the two pastors, I began working through the steps, and the Woman to Woman Mentoring Ministry was born.

God is perpetually at work in a believer's life, whether or not we recognize him. I firmly believe there are no coincidences, only God incidences and divine appointments. When I hear people speak of serendipity, I kindly reply that it was God, not karma or chance.

God was getting me just where he wanted me. He took an ordinary person through the process of doing something extraordinary—starting an international mentoring ministry for women. My role was to hear and recognize his still, small voice and sense his presence in all the doors opening to start the ministry . . . trust . . . and obey.

In the Bible, a covenant is an agreement or vow between God and his people, in which God makes promises to his people and requires certain conduct from them. "Moses told the leaders of the Israelite tribes, 'This is what the LORD has commanded: When a man makes a vow to the LORD or swears an oath to put himself under an obligation, he must not break his word; he must do whatever he has promised'" (Num. 30:1–2 HCSB).

Today, covenants usually require a written agreement from each party to abide by the specifics of the agreement. But some are verbal, like marriage vows and the vow I made to the Lord when he said, "Feed my sheep," and I said, "Okay." It's been over twenty years since I made that covenant with the Lord. I'm still feeding his sheep, and he's still bringing sheep for me to feed.

Your Memories

Raini and I both recognized God's presence in getting our attention and directing us to follow the plans he had for each of us to start a ministry. Maybe God hasn't called you to start a ministry, but you've sensed his presence in your life in other areas—work, relationships, parenting, ministry, finding the right place to live, or meeting the right mate.

In the previous chapter, Recognizing God's Voice, you identified an occasion when you heard God's still, small voice. Perhaps you didn't actually *hear* an audible sound, but you knew it was God—then you sensed his presence in the details or the way the incident progressed. Or maybe you never thought before about God being in that circumstance. Often we take credit ourselves or assign it to others like doctors, lawyers, parents, teachers, spouses, even pastors. Look back now and try to identify God's presence in that situation. You now know it was God working behind the scenes.

Ways to Remember God's Goodness— *Looking for God*...

For the next three weeks, look for God in *everything* you do and in *every* circumstance: God-moments where you sense God's presence. Note them here and date your entries. It's been said it takes three weeks to form a habit, so if you do this faithfully, you'll be well on your way to recognizing God at work and noticing how good God is *all* the time.

God used me to encourage "J." o to pray for her.

Let's Pray

Dear Lord, replace my constant searching for plausible and reasonable causes for my circumstances with the reminder to look for you in the circumstances. Humble me so I don't take credit for my accomplishments or give others glory belonging to you and you alone. Wake up my senses to your presence and keep me mindful of how you are present in all the ordinary and extraordinary happenings in my day. Give me a sense of bumping into you at every turn. Knock me over if you need to get my attention. I promise to be looking for you around every corner. Amen.

Talk about It

1. Share a circumstance where you know it had to be God involved in the outcome. How did you know it was God? Did you give him the glory?

Soccer shoes, Makayla, our house, my jobs + people God brought.

2. Now remember a milestone moment in your life when you *didn't* recognize God at work. How do you now see it was God? How will remembering God's presence in a past situation help you recognize him in the future?

Moving to middlefield (now not Orwell) mom is close to us) He knows the future - I can trust Him

51

3. What covenants or vows have you made? Did both parties honor the agreement? Did you? *Yes*

Marriage vows

4. In Deuteronomy 29:2–6, Moses reminds the Israelites they saw and couldn't ignore God's presence, and yet they still didn't understand or appreciate God. Read these verses and then compare them to the forgetfulness of God's presence in the world today.

Moses summoned all the Israelites and said to them:

Your eyes have seen all that the LORD did in Egypt to Pharaoh, to all his officials and to all his land. With your own eyes you saw those great trials, those signs and great wonders. But to this day the LORD has not given you a mind that understands or eyes that see or ears that hear. Yet the LORD says, "During the forty years that I led you through the wilderness, your clothes did not wear out, nor did the sandals on your feet. . . . I did this so that you might know that I am the LORD your God." (Deut. 29:2–6)

God, You are so good to give us gracious glimpses of your presence & power in our lives. Help me to have eyes to see You at work each and NOT day take You for granted, Blessed, Holy One!

Chapter Three

Recognizing His Intervention

Then the LORD said, "I am making a covenant with you. Before all your people I will do wonders never before done in any nation in all the world. The people you live among will see how awesome is the work that I, the LORD, will do for you."

—Exodus 34:10

No one can feel inferior and futile when the sovereign Lord keeps intervening. A history of redemption allows people to define themselves not by their enslaved past but by their liberated future.

—Chris Tiegreen[1]

Bible Memories

Moses reminds the Israelites of God's intervention in the past and his covenant to intervene and protect them in the future, as they move to possess the land he was giving them:

> You're going to think to yourselves, "Oh! We're out-numbered ten to one by these nations! We'll never even make a dent in them!" But I'm telling you, Don't be afraid. Remember, yes, remember in detail what GOD, your God, did to Pharaoh and all Egypt. Remember the great contests to which you were eyewitnesses: the

miracle-signs, the wonders, GOD's mighty hand as he
stretched out his arm and took you out of there. GOD,
your God, is going to do the same thing to these people
you're now so afraid of. (Deut. 7:17–19 *The Message*)

God had intervened to protect them from Pharaoh—the plagues,
their miraculous escape from Egypt, and the parting of the Red Sea
for them to cross before it closed back to drown all of Pharaoh's
soldiers—and God had intervened in *every* aspect of their newly
gained freedom. They had seen things only God could have done.
So Moses reassured the people that God would continue protecting them against any enemy they encountered in Canaan. Moses
beseeched them to "remember in detail" everything they had seen
the Lord do to free and protect them. Why would they think he
would abandon them now?

But they were a forgetful people. Moses *repeatedly* reminded
the people of God's past interventions on their behalf because he
knew that as soon as they forgot about them, they would start
fearing for their safety and stop trusting God. And that's exactly
what happened, *repeatedly*.

Laurie Winslow Sargent Remembers God's Goodness

Laurie Winslow Sargent understands the significance of docu-
menting God's intervention "in detail" for the next generation to
know God's goodness. Maybe someone will come to know the
Lord for the first time by reading an account of something only
God could do.

I mostly write self-help parenting nonfiction, but I also
write true stories of God's faithfulness and miraculous
answers to prayer. I wish I'd learned earlier how to

balance time in writing both. As I age, I feel a pressing responsibility to get all those true stories written down for family members who don't know God and for others who might discover a deeper faith from reading them.

On my eventual deathbed, leaving some of those God-stories unwritten would cause me more chagrin than leaving my latest nonfiction book unfinished. God puts some events in my life because he wants—or expects—me to write about them.

Retelling of God's interventions makes them gifts that keep on giving. A friend once said in reference to the unusual ways God answers my prayers: "You lead a charmed life." I objected. I believe when an event points to God and I boldly tell or write about it, he simply gives me more to tell.

Other believers have as many God-experiences as I do, but by not telling about or writing down the experience, they don't remember what God has done or his intervention in their lives. When we forget God's gifts of mercy, our faith dwindles. I often forget, too, and then I find one of my old stories leading me to praise him again and pray with more faith for the next great thing.

My Memories

My husband and I lead a support group for parents and grandparents of prodigals. Most participants start the group discouraged, burdened, hopeless, fearful, sometimes angry, and often feeling abandoned by God in their heartache over their wayward child.

At the end of each meeting, we ask for prayer requests, and each member writes down his or her prayer requests and the requests of others in the group. The requests are often for specific ways they want God to intervene in their child's life. Each member documents and dates the prayer requests so we can pray for each other.

As the group progresses over the weeks, we ask for praises or updates on how things are going with their prodigals. Often as a member relates a story, maybe not one he or she feels is particularly encouraging, another group member will remind him or her that this was an earlier prayer request. The reminder shocks the parent or grandparent because he or she forgot about asking God to intervene in that situation, or didn't recognize it was God: "It's so hard remembering to recognize God's intervention and not just attribute it to circumstances or coincidence."

Maybe they expected God to answer in a different way, so they overlooked his glorious intervention—his way. They missed seeing God's mighty hand in the situation, but sharing their prayer request with others who wrote it down helps them claim a victory.

Sometimes we overlook God's intervention because we're expecting him to fix everything or make a grandiose gesture, instead of praising him for the baby steps along the way. I remember a specific example where we had prayed that a child would be "surrounded by Christians." When the parent told us her daughter's new sister-in-law was a Christian, I reminded her she had asked us to pray for God to surround her daughter with Christians. Her first response was, "Oh, but I wanted *lots* of Christians around her." I assured her God did intervene and answer her prayer—it only takes one person.

Your Memories

Instead of worrying about how God is intervening or why he isn't intervening the way you think he should, recognize that he is setting the stage for *his* purpose and plan. You don't have to be an author to remember in detail or write down the many wonders you see God do as he intervenes in the circumstances of your life. Think of a time you asked God specifically to intervene in a situation, and that situation turned out well, maybe even better than you expected. Did you remember to thank God and attribute the victory to him, or were you just happy things went the way you wanted?

Describe the situation here, and if you haven't given God the credit already for his intervention, do so now.

Ways to Remember God's Goodness—
Prayer and Praise Journal ....

Start a Prayer and Praise Journal. You can use the one included in the Appendix, or you can use it as a pattern to make your own in a notebook or journal of your choice. Date and document your prayer requests. Once a week, review your prayer requests, and in the praise column, note when and how God answered your requests. You'll be amazed at how often and consistently God intervenes in your life. Prayer isn't to remind God about your problems, but to remind you to ask him to intervene. Praise reminds you to thank God for his goodness!

Let's Pray

Lord, I know you're intervening in my life and want the best for me, and I should not fear or doubt. Remind me to thank you and be grateful for your continued goodness. Keep me from becoming stiff-necked and turning to other solutions rather than asking you to intervene . . . and remind me to acknowledge your perfect will and plans for each situation. Help me learn how to document my prayer requests and recognize and praise your answers. Amen.

Talk about It

1. How does Deuteronomy 7:17–19 encourage you to look for and remember God's interventions?

> God is still bigger than my circumstances and He will make a way how He chooses

2. Why do you think we miss God's intervention?

> It's not what we were expecting - We stopped looking for His response

3. How will a Prayer and Praise Journal help you recognize and remember God's interventions? How will you remember to use it?

> It will cause me to be more intentional in my prayer life

4. In what current situation would you like to see God intervene?

> my attitude (marriage)
> &
> health
> finances (get ahead)
> tithing
> His answers

Chapter Four

Recognizing
His Omnipotence

The LORD answered Moses, "Is the LORD's arm too short? Now you will see whether or not what I say will come true for you."
—Numbers 11:23

Eventually, you will learn to relax and enjoy the adventure of our journey together. As long as you stay close to Me, My sovereign Presence protects you wherever you go.

—Sarah Young[1]

Bible Memories

The omnipotence of God is his absolute, unlimited power and supremacy. Other words often used to describe this characteristic, which only God possesses, are *sovereign* and *almighty*. He is the Alpha and Omega, the beginning and the end. He knows all, sees all, oversees all, and is everywhere at once. Nothing takes God by surprise. He is always in control and the ultimate authority. In Numbers 33, God instructs Moses to write down the stages of the Israelites' journey out of Egypt. This chapter is a concise recorded timeline of the supremacy of God guiding and leading his people:

> Here are the stages in the journey of the Israelites
> when they came out of Egypt by divisions under the

leadership of Moses and Aaron. At the LORD's command Moses recorded the stages in their journey. This is their journey by stages:

The Israelites set out from Rameses on the fifteenth day of the first month, the day after the Passover. They marched out defiantly in full view of all the Egyptians, who were burying all their firstborn, whom the LORD had struck down among them; for the LORD had brought judgment on their gods.

The Israelites left Rameses and camped at Sukkoth.

They left Sukkoth and camped at Etham, on the edge of the desert.

They left Etham, turned back to Pi Hahiroth, to the east of Baal Zephon, and camped near Migdol.

They left Pi Hahiroth and passed through the sea into the desert, and when they had traveled for three days in the Desert of Etham, they camped at Marah. (Num. 33:1–8)

I included verses 1 through 8 with the passing through the Red Sea, but you might like to stop now and read in your Bible the remaining forty-seven verses of Moses's recording of their journey.

Why would God ask Moses to chronicle the Israelites' journey? So they would remember their travels and experiences and could recognize God's omnipotence and sovereignty in overseeing every detail of their ethnic history—now recorded in the Bible forever.

Reading about their journey can get confusing and seem like the Israelites were wandering aimlessly. It's true the journey from Egypt to Moab should only have taken a couple of weeks, but because of the freed generation's forgetfulness and disobedience, God purposely had the trip take four decades while they grew old and died—they were not going to see the Promised Land. Only their children and grandchildren would have that privilege.

Just as you would retrace the places you went on a trip and the experiences of your adventure, this concise timeline in Numbers 33 shows God's powerful hand in the Israelites' travels through barren wilderness, provision of food from heaven, protection from other tribes, and God's omnipotent care even while disciplining them.

They didn't have maps, compasses, or a GPS. God was always in charge of their humbling journey, but they often forgot he was the one in control.

Beth Willis Miller Remembers God's Goodness

Beth Willis Miller felt like she was aimlessly wandering through life, forgetting the omnipotence of God. Just as God had Moses write a timeline of the Israelites' journey, Beth found renewed faith in God as she retraced her own life's journey.

I participated with my husband and daughter in a low-impact family ropes course with a series of challenges we had to solve together as a team. At the end, the facilitator gathered us in a circle and asked if we wanted the final debriefing questions to be spiritual. We said, "Yes!" So he asked, "On a scale of one to five, with five being as close to God as possible, where are you?"

I don't remember what anyone else said, but I'll never forget what I said: "I'm a one." It was an epiphany. I had accepted Jesus Christ as my Lord and Savior at the age of ten during a revival. I remember my fingers forming a heart as I sat on the front pew after filling out the decision card. I grew in my knowledge of Jesus Christ through Sunday school, missions organizations, and memorizing Scripture.

Yet, here I was, a busy wife and working mother feeling like a "one." How did I get here? Jesus hadn't moved, but I felt far away from him. Later that same week, I heard this song ("I Miss My Time with You") by Larnelle Harris: "I miss my time with you, those moments together, I need to be with you each day and it hurts me when you say you're too busy."

A sudden realization began a time of transformation. I knew in my heart that prayer, time in God's Word, and worship with my fellow believers were the choices I needed to make to change my "one" to a "five." Our family began attending church again and I enrolled in one Bible study after another. As part of Beth Moore's *Believing God* Bible study, we completed a timeline of our life in ten-year segments, asking God to reveal to us all the spiritual mile markers in our lives . . . broken places, hurts, disappointments, accomplishments, and joyful times . . . to help us remember God had been there all along and his grace is sufficient.

I created a timeline for each decade of my life. Completing this timeline helped get my thoughts on paper, and God used this process to heal me in many ways.

The Hebrew concept of time is like a person rowing a boat—facing your past as you back into the future. God has been with me all along. I'm not stuck in the past. I'm proactively rowing into the future, moving forward with my focus, my mindset, on God's sovereignty. He sees the past, the present, and the future all at once. He is omnipotent. This I will never forget.

My Memories

I accepted Jesus as my Lord and Savior at the age of eleven, the year after the murder of my father in the line of duty as a California highway patrolman. A camp counselor at a youth camp asked a life-changing question: "I know you've lost your earthly father, but would you like a heavenly Father who will never leave or forsake you?"

I stayed on fire for the Lord even through debilitating scoliosis that kept me home from school in a plaster body cast for two years. I attended church faithfully and had a close relationship with the Lord until my senior year in college, when I started dating a nonbeliever and married him the day after graduation. We divorced six years later, and I became a single, working mom.

As I view my life timeline, I recognize God never let go of me, even as I ran from him after my divorce and during a time of rebellious backsliding. I see my life before knowing God . . . after knowing God . . . backsliding and running from God . . . rededicating my life to God . . . and now victoriously serving God. I still encounter life's problems, like prodigal children, blending a family, and breast cancer, but I recognize God's omnipotence. I remember that God is in control and everything he allows into a believer's life has a purpose that he will use for good.

Your Memories

God can use every experience in our lives—the good, the bad, the ugly—to accomplish his sovereign purposes: "And we know that in all things God works for the good of those who love him, who have been called according to his purpose" (Rom. 8:28). When we surrender our hearts, souls, and thoughts to God, we're giving him ultimate, unlimited, absolute power in our lives. The problem is we foolishly want to reclaim some of that power or help him out a bit, which doesn't work well because God sees our lives from an omnipotent perspective, and we're limited to our finite view.

Can you remember a time when you thought God's power was limited—his arm was too short to reach the heart of your problem? You just knew he wouldn't be able to change a certain person or situation, so you gave up or tried to take control yourself. How did that work for you?

Now reframe the situation acknowledging God's sovereignty. For example, "Even though my marriage is troubled, God is bigger than our troubles. He hasn't forgotten about us, and he wants us to remember the vows we took before him. He will work things out for the good of our marriage and those who are watching us."

Now try reframing your problem:

Ways to Remember God's Goodness— Creating a Life Timeline .... ✐

Carol Kent has a tagline that captures the essence and value of remembering life experiences: "*Minutes* become *marker moments* that turn into *memories* that feed our passions, stir our dreams, ignite our creativity, and demand a response."

Have you thought about your life journey in terms of marker moments on a timeline before? Like Beth Willis Miller and Moses, create a chronological life timeline by using the form on the next page. Focus on ten-year periods, and then break those down into years if you want more detail. Pray and ask God to help you remember significant life events—marker moments—broken places, hurts, disappointments, accomplishments, and joyful times. Then go back and delineate where you see God's almighty power at work or where you tried relying on your own weaker resources.

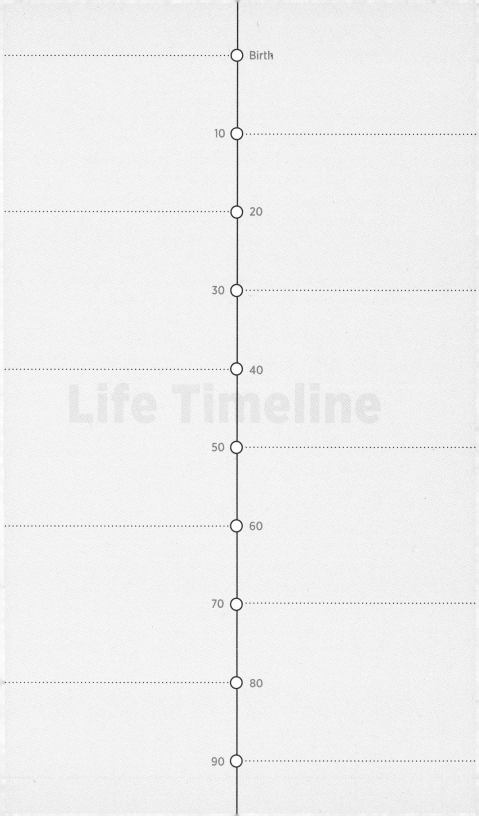

Let's Pray

Beth Willis Miller wrote this prayer: Lord Jesus, give me a heart so yearning for your presence that only a few days without time in prayer and in your Word seem like an eternity. Give me a heart motivated by a desire for you, not for what you do for me. Help me take what you've made known to me and make you known to others. I want a heart where your name and renown is my deepest desire. Let me feel your Holy Spirit woo me once again to the place where I meet you. In the simplicity of my prayer time, grant me a heart confronted by the majesty of my Redeemer—the One responsible for any good in me. I bow at your Cross. I experience anew your forgiveness, redemption, mercy, and grace, as I sense your blood dripping over the Crown of Thorns pressed into your brow onto my heart, covering my sin. I get up from my knees wearing your robe of righteousness, as I face the day ahead. Welcoming your fresh mercies, which fall like manna from heaven, my heart is moved once again. I surrender all. Morning after morning. Amen.

Talk about It

1. Do you see God as omnipotent in your life? Why or why not?

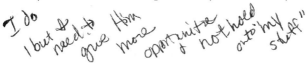

2. How did creating your life timeline help you realize and remember more of God's sovereignty and goodness in your life?

3. In the opening verse, Numbers 11:23, the Lord challenges Moses's doubts as to whether God could really provide enough meat for the six hundred thousand Israelites. The Holman Christian Standard

Bible translates "Is my arm too short?" as "Is the LORD's power limited?" Discuss how the following verses assure you God's arm is always long enough and his power is endless.

> So do not fear, for I am with you; do not be dismayed, for I am your God. I will strengthen you and help you; I will uphold you with my righteous right hand. (Isa. 41:10)

> If I rise on the wings of the dawn, if I settle on the far side of the sea, even there your hand will guide me, your right hand will hold me fast. (Ps. 139:9–10)

4. In Beth's story, she was a 1 on a scale where 5 was the closest to God. Where would you place yourself? If you're below a 4, what steps can you take to draw closer to God? Would remembering God's goodness help?

keep in mind that my emotions arent an honest indicator of my rel. to Him – be real + surrender to Him, trust His word, watch Him be faithful.

67

Section Two

Honoring
God

*I will honor those who honor me,
and I will despise those who think lightly of me.*

—1 Samuel 2:30b NLT

*God's inherent glory is what he possesses because he is God. . . .
But we are commanded to recognize his glory, honor his glory,
declare his glory, praise his glory, reflect his glory, and live for his
glory. . . . We owe him every honor we can possibly give.*

—Rick Warren[1]

Remembering God is synonymous with honoring God. We cannot honor someone or something forgotten. Honor is not a word commonly used today—to society's detriment—since honor connotes respect, esteem, reverence, and awe. We're a generation where positions of status that should command honor and esteem are the brunt of jokes on late-night talk shows, and then the people in those positions become guests on the same shows that degrade them.

Our great God deserves our honor and respect, and the psalmists understood God's *majesty* . . . another word not commonly heard today. Psalm 77, written by Asaph, one of David's chief musicians, is the scriptural foundation for this section. You might want to turn now to Psalm 77 in your Bible and read the entire psalm, and then linger in the Book of Psalms. The psalmists frequently write about our predisposition to forget God, but they also emphasize God *never* forgets us.

Chapter Five

Honoring His Greatness

How great is God—beyond our understanding!

—Job 36:26a

Thinking about what God has done isn't a trip down memory lane where we sit with a box of Kleenex and get ready to sniffle as nostalgia overcomes us. . . . God wants us to remember for more important reasons—so that we might grow in faith, trust, and commitment to Him every time we are reminded of His greatness.

—Poppy Smith[1]

Bible Memories

In Psalm 77:1–6a, the psalmist is greatly distressed, and like many going through hard times, nighttime is the worst. Darkness ushers in doubts, fears, and worries about past, present, and future concerns; however, it can also be a prayerful time to remember how our Great God has helped us in the past and won't forget us now. Courage is fear overcome by prayer.

> I cried out to God for help;
>> I cried out to God to hear me.
> When I was in distress, I sought the Lord;

> at night I stretched out untiring hands,
> and I would not be comforted.
>
> I remembered you, God, and I groaned;
> I meditated, and my spirit grew faint.
> You kept my eyes from closing;
> I was too troubled to speak.
> I thought about the former days,
> the years of long ago;
> I remembered my songs in the night.

When the Israelites were suffering and groaning for four hundred and thirty years under the cruel treatment of the Egyptians, they must have thought God had forgotten the promises he made to their deceased forefathers. God's covenant promised he would multiply Abraham, Isaac, and Jacob's descendants into a great nation.

They didn't recognize that God *was* multiplying them during their captivity. Only Jacob's family of seventy originally went to Egypt (Gen. 46:27); "But the Israelites were exceedingly fruitful; they multiplied greatly, increased in numbers and became so numerous that the land was filled with them" (Exod. 1:7). God grew seventy people into a lineage "as numerous as the stars in the sky" (Deut. 10:22); but it wasn't how they envisioned God growing them.

Exodus 2:24–25 confirms, "God heard their groaning and he remembered his covenant with Abraham, with Isaac and with Jacob. So God looked on the Israelites and was concerned about them." At the perfect time, when they had become a formidable people group, God set them free, and he wanted them to remember that night in honor of his greatness.

> Now the length of time the Israelite people lived in
> Egypt was 430 years. At the end of the 430 years, to the
> very day, all the LORD's divisions left Egypt. Because the
> LORD kept vigil that night to bring them out of Egypt,

on this night all the Israelites are to keep vigil to honor the LORD for the generations to come. (Exod. 12:40–42)

Often we see the most growth in our spiritual lives during hard times, when God is growing us spiritually and emotionally. We may think he has forgotten us, but God is good and God is great. He never forgets his promises to his people even though his people often forget their promises to him.

Nancy Remembers God's Goodness

I heard Nancy's inspiring testimony at a women's event at our church. Today, Nancy honors God by leading the children's ministry at church and helping the next generation learn about the greatness of God.

I have no special talent that sets me apart from anyone else. What isn't ordinary is my salvation—a life-changing experience I will never forget.

When I was young, I went to Sunday school and loved it. Then my father received a transfer and our family moved to Italy. We didn't go back to church until I was a senior in high school. By then, I wanted *nothing* to do with church. I took control of my life to live it *my* way. I no longer believed Bible stories. Fairy tales. I was past agnostic, heading fast to atheist.

I married my dear Bill and we had an adored son, Erik. Bill's career was going great and we bought a lovely home, made friends, entertained, and thoroughly enjoyed our life. I was twenty-nine years old and everything was perfect, except I was afraid of going to sleep.

Nighttime brought fear—absolute terror. I was terrified of death, thinking we would become nothing. I understood the body decaying, but I knew I was more than just a body. What about the *real* me? Is that gone, too? Every night when I closed my eyes, these thoughts enveloped me as I cried myself to sleep.

Until one desperate night, I got up, walked to the railing of the loft, and prayed the world's most pathetic prayer: "God, I don't really think you're real; I don't think you're there. But if you are real, I want to know the truth. Show yourself to me and I will follow you."

Suddenly, everything changed! All the fear, doubts, terror, despair, disbelief . . . gone. No blinding lights or audible voice from heaven, but it was a true "road to Damascus" experience. I didn't know then about the road to Damascus or how science could date the Earth at billions of years old or how the animals all fit on the ark. I didn't care. What I knew was God is *real!* I belonged to him and I would follow him. I experienced the most incredible, indescribable peace.

The next morning, I turned on the TV (not my practice), and a preacher was explaining salvation through our precious Jesus. I prayed with the preacher, but I knew God had received me the night before. I now understood God was loving and powerful. I wanted to experience God's greatness daily. Not only find out *about* him, but also find him *personally.*

God continually answers that request by filling me with his presence. He manifests himself in so many ways. It's an exciting adventure and honor to follow him and to teach the little children about my Great God, my Father, and my Lord.

My Memories

My husband and I were going to watch our three grandchildren at our home several times during a two-month period, when due to clerical issues, the kids wouldn't have health insurance. We live in a rural area without a nearby emergency room or urgent care. Initially, I was fearful and worried one of the kids might get hurt or sick while on our watch. What would we do?

Then I remembered our Great God cared about my precious grandchildren, and he provided greater protection than any insurance company did. So I asked our small groups to pray for our grandchildren to remain well and accident-free—at home and at our house—during that two-month period. We prayed with the kids about it, too.

Before we knew it, the two months passed and each child remained well and uninjured. My husband and I then reminded the grandkids and their parents that all the honor and glory for their safety went to God, and we needed to thank him for watching over the kids. How easy it is to ask God for something, and then when he displays his greatness and all goes well, we're happy about it but forget to give God the honor he is due.

Your Memories

Do you have worries and fears that haunt you at night and prevent restful sleep? Does Satan use the quiet and darkness of the night to terrorize you? Is there one recurring fear? Let's deal with that today so Satan can never use it against you again. Close your eyes and let your mind go briefly to the fearful thought or memory. Then ask God in his infinite greatness to take away that fear and never let it disturb you again. Remember how God has rescued you in the past—after all, you're still here—and trust he will honor his promise: "Because God has said, 'Never will I leave you; never will I forsake you'" (Heb. 13:5b).

In the future, if you experience a familiar sinking feeling in your stomach, and your heart races in the grip of fear and panic, remember this moment and how you turned everything over to God, knowing he is greater than any person, place, or thing. Make a note here describing the peace you now feel so you can revisit it if you begin feeling anxious in the future.

Ways to Remember God's Goodness— *Ridding Yourself of Bad Memories* ....

Most of us have more than one bad memory that plagues us as we rehearse in our mind past failures, mistakes, or traumas. A tangible and memorable way to cast out past hurts, hang-ups, and bad memories is to make a list of them. Then pray over the list and ask God in his ultimate greatness to remove these from your mind. Set a match to the list, or put it into a fireplace, and watch it burn. Every time your mind tries to return to any of these memories, remember them turning into ashes.

If you're not in a place where you can burn your list, write the list here and then put a big X over it.

Let's Pray

Lord, you are so great and worthy of my honor and trust. Forgive me for the times I let fear, worry, and doubt slip into my heart. Give me courage to face my giants and to seek your help in overcoming any foe—physical or spiritual. Remind me of how great you truly are and remind me to give you all the glory and honor you deserve for freeing me from fear and bad memories. Help me rest and live in your perfect peace. You are my great and holy God. Amen.

Talk about It

1. How has accepting Christ as your Lord and Savior helped rid you of fears and doubts?

2. You may have sung lyrics similar to these in church: "How great is our God? Sing with me, how great is our God? And all the world will see how great, how great is our God!"[2] How does publically giving God glory and honor for his goodness in our lives help others recognize his greatness? Why do we often forget to talk about the greatness of our God?

3. Discuss how to apply current events to Moses's plea in Deuteronomy 3:24–25:

> Sovereign LORD, you have begun to show to your servant your greatness and your strong hand. For what god is there in heaven or on earth who can do the deeds and mighty works you do? Let me go over and see the

good land beyond the Jordan—that fine hill country and Lebanon.

4. Deuteronomy 3:26–27 was God's answer to Moses's plea. What were the consequences of Moses not recognizing and honoring the greatness of God's power when he told Moses to *speak* to the rock for water? How could this apply to our world not honoring God today?

> But because of you [Israelites] the LORD was angry with me [Moses] and would not listen to me. "That is enough," the LORD said. "Do not speak to me anymore about this matter. Go up to the top of Pisgah and look west and north and south and east. Look at the land with your own eyes, since you are not going to cross this Jordan."

Chapter Six

Honoring His Glory

So the sisters sent word to Jesus, "Lord, the one you love is sick."
When he heard this, Jesus said, "This sickness will not end in
death. No, it is for God's glory so that God's Son may be glorified
through it."

—John 11:3-4

It's always up to God how He answers prayer so that His great
glory can be displayed.

—Heidi Williams

Bible Memories

Webster's Dictionary defines *honoring* as: to regard or treat (someone) with admiration and respect—to regard or treat with *honor*.
And: to give special recognition to—to confer *honor* on. Webster's
Dictionary defines *glory* as: praise, honor, or distinction extended
by common consent—renown. And: worshipful praise, honor, and
thanksgiving—giving *glory* to God.

God often orchestrates circumstances so the witnesses of his
great feat will attribute honor and glory to him. Like when he told
the Israelites to camp by the sea so Pharaoh would think he had
them trapped between the desert and the Red Sea, but God had
a plan: "'I will harden Pharaoh's heart, and he will pursue them.

But I will gain glory for myself through Pharaoh and all his army, and the Egyptians will know that I am the LORD.' So the Israelites did this" (Exod. 14:4). Understandably, they must have wondered how God was going to get them out of what seemed like a hopeless situation. But Moses assured the people:

> Do not be afraid. Stand firm and you will see the deliverance the LORD will bring you today. The Egyptians you see today you will never see again. The LORD will fight for you; you need only to be still. (Exod. 14:13–14)

When Israel went through difficult times, remembering, meditating on, and honoring God's goodness to them in the past helped them withstand the current hardships. They knew in their hearts God was capable and trustworthy and deserved all the glory for all he had done for them. They had seen his glory prevail on numerous occasions, even though they often forgot and needed constant reminding. Remembering gave them hope, as it did for Asaph in Psalm 77:7–12, and as it should for you and me.

> Will the Lord reject forever?
> Will he never show his favor again?
> Has his unfailing love vanished forever?
> Has his promise failed for all time?
> Has God forgotten to be merciful?
> Has he in anger withheld his compassion?
>
> Then I thought, "To this I will appeal:
> the years when the Most High stretched out his
> right hand.
> I will remember the deeds of the LORD;
> yes, I will remember your miracles of long ago.
> I will consider all your works
> and meditate on all your mighty deeds."

The memory of God's goodness—his miraculous deeds and past miracles—was what Asaph decided to meditate on and think about instead of current problems and trials. He would give God the glory for the things God had done and was yet to do. We need to do the same . . . just be still and let God be God.

Dianne Barker Remembers God's Goodness

Dianne was having a very bad day, but remembering God's goodness during past trials and her willingness to give God the glory no matter how the events turned out gave her peace.

Several years ago, we experienced a difficult, unforgettable month. Things couldn't get any worse . . . I thought. My husband and I walked in the door, emotionally drained after a four-week nightmare dealing with my bipolar brother. Drenched with exhaustion, James and I drew a long breath of relief as we arrived home. The phone's blinking light indicated a message: "Mom and Dad, now don't worry. But call me as soon as you can."

It was a message from our son calling from overseas where he'd spent a year in ministry. The international call to him connected quickly, and our son explained he had an infected boil on his hip. The doctor warned it probably would require surgery.

Surgery! In a foreign country! I fought the visuals wrestling on my mind's screen. "Should we go?" We'd updated our passports—in case of an emergency.

No. The rest of his group would continue traveling while he stayed behind with a family connected with the ministry. He was receiving excellent care.

Nearly frozen with anxiety, James and I managed to get to the midweek prayer service at church where praying friends would share our burden, making it bearable. Many offered consolation and assured us of their love and prayers. One concerned friend voiced my unspoken fear, "He could lose his leg!"

God! My heart cried the name of the One who held all my hope.

Preparing for bed, expecting no sleep and sobbing violently, I heard a quiet voice: *If he loses his leg, it will be for my greater glory.* I remembered a conversation with my teenage daughter years ago after God had answered a prayer exactly the way we'd prayed. I said, "God is good!" Her wise reply: "God is good, whether or not he does what we ask. If this hadn't turned out well, God is still good." It was a reminder that my circumstances don't alter his goodness. Wrapped in a blanket of calm, I dried my tears and slept.

I acknowledged God's goodness with praise when our son's wound didn't require surgery and he rejoined his mission team. A heart-wrenching circumstance had a happy ending.

What influenced my life most was not the *outcome*, but the peace God gave *in the midst* of the circumstance. This ordeal gave me a new life perspective: *whatever* God allows in my life—even if it doesn't *look* good—he will use for my good and his greater glory.

My Memories

Every author experiences disappointment and rejection: times when you wonder if God has forgotten you or doesn't want you to continue writing. Why did that publisher keep my proposal for a year and then tell me they aren't going to publish my book after all? Or why did a book that was helping so many go out of print?

Why doesn't a publisher pick up the book I'm sure God wants written? These are the discouraging thoughts that can keep an author tossing and turning at night and uninspired during the day. Remembering I'm writing for God's glory helps me through all those uncertain and "why" times. He has a plan, and if I continue to pray and turn my writing over to him, everything will turn out to further his kingdom in the way and timing he knows is best.

In the Preface, I mentioned that *Forsaken God?* has been on my heart since 2006. I wrote other books in the interim and stayed optimistic that if God wanted this book written, he would determine the time and the publisher. My job was to stay persistent, remember his favor with previous publishers, and give him *all* the glory when one day it was on bookshelves and electronic readers. So today, I give God the glory for you having *Forsaken God?* available to read and study.

Your Memories

Think of something you desperately wanted God to do in your life, but he didn't do it for many years. When it finally happened, did you remember asking God for it? Did you take credit for it, or did you give God the glory? If you took credit at the time, can you now see how it was God's timing all along? Take a moment here to honor God by acknowledging the good result was all about him and not about you.

Ways to Remember God's Goodness—
Giving God the Glory He Deserves

For the next three weeks, every time something goes the way you want it to go, verbally give God the glory, and make a note of it here. When something turns out differently than you hoped, still give God the glory, knowing he has a better plan. You should start seeing a pattern to remember—when you give God the glory no matter what, you experience *peace*. When you don't give God the glory, you experience *pride* or *pain*.

Let's Pray

Lord, I want to show you honor by giving you the glory in all circumstances, but that doesn't come naturally. My ego often takes credit for the good that happens, and my emotions are disappointed in you when things don't turn out the way I want. Help me show you honor and give you the glory always . . . no matter what. Amen.

Talk about It

1. Using the definitions for honor and glory in the Bible Memories section, discuss how giving glory to God honors him.

2. Why is it so difficult for us to give God glory when things don't go the way we want?

3. The opening verses of this chapter, John 11:3–4, state that Lazarus wouldn't die. Yet Jesus delayed coming for three days and Lazarus did die. Many observed Jesus bring Lazarus back to life (John 11:3–45). How did Jesus's delay bring him more glory than arriving before Lazarus died? How have you seen a delay in your life turn out to be a good thing? Did you give God glory?

4. How does giving God the glory keep us humble?

Chapter Seven

Honoring His Wonders and Miracles

Many, LORD my God,
are the wonders you have done,
the things you planned for us.
None can compare with you;
were I to speak and tell of your deeds,
they would be too many to declare.

—Psalm 40:5

"Oh Jesus, thank you for my miracle." Crisp and clear as the air
itself, Jesus whispered back something I'll never forget: "Ema,
thank you for accepting my miracle."

—Ema McKinley[1]

Bible Memories

God visibly displayed many signs and wonders in biblical times. Even though Pharaoh's Egyptian gods tried to match the power of the Israelites' God, each of the plagues God brought on the Egyptians forced them to recognize that the God of the Israelites was in control. No other god or magician could compete with the One who parted the Red Sea while the Israelites walked through on dry ground. God Almighty could, and did, free them from the tyranny of the Egyptians. Moses continually reminded the people,

"He is the one you praise; he is your God, who performed for you those great and awesome wonders you saw with your own eyes" (Deut. 10:21).

Down through the generations the prophets, psalmists, disciples, and apostles told the stories . . . over and over . . . of God's miracles and wonders so the people would never forget and always honor God's astounding goodness to them; but they did forget . . . over and over. However, the psalmist remembered:

> Your ways, God, are holy.
> > What god is as great as our God?
> You are the God who performs miracles;
> > you display your power among the peoples.
> With your mighty arm you redeemed your people,
> > the descendants of Jacob and Joseph.
>
> The waters saw you, God,
> > the waters saw you and writhed;
> > the very depths were convulsed.
> The clouds poured down water,
> > the heavens resounded with thunder;
> > your arrows flashed back and forth.
> Your thunder was heard in the whirlwind,
> > your lightning lit up the world;
> > the earth trembled and quaked. (Ps. 77:13–18)

The God of past miracles is the same God of today's miracles. His wondrous ways should still command our awed respect. Look for miracles in your life and in the world around you. Remember them and tell the spectacular, miraculous stories of God's goodness over and over!

Heidi Williams Remembers God's Goodness

Heidi Williams gives God *all* the glory for her amazing miracle. She also looks for daily reminders of God's miracles we often take for granted in God's glorious creation.

My husband has had a series of medical problems related to a degenerative disc and joint disease resulting in surgeries, injections, and numerous procedures. After one surgery, he developed a staph infection requiring two subsequent surgeries. Sitting alone in the waiting room in the middle of the night, I was fearful and anxious of becoming a young, single mother and widow.

After four hours, I remember the surgeon knelt down and took a deep breath before explaining the gravity of the situation and the complicated and lengthy procedures ahead of Roger. He asked, "Does Roger have a living will? Do you have medical directives in the event he's put on life support?"

I closed my eyes and began to pray, "Lord, I know you have him in the hands of a great physician, but Father, *you* are *the great physician.* I place him in your hands completely and I trust your will, not my will, for our lives." My anxious thoughts turned to peace. I knew I was not alone. Jesus was there and the power of the Holy Spirit, my Counselor, quickened my heart with the peace that passes all understanding. As I touched Roger's face and stroked his cheek, I praised God for the gift of unconditional love and the beautiful memories we had made together.

Then, to everyone's amazement, the following morning the doctor announced, "Well, it's a miracle! The staph infection is gone. There's no evidence of it in his bones or bloodstream, and we're going to release him to go home."

We had witnessed a modern-day miracle! Whether Roger lived or went to be with Jesus, I knew it would be God's will. I believe in miracles and I believe in the power of prayer and praise, but I know God controls the outcome. Either scenario, still I would praise him.

Miracles don't just happen in incredible stories like ours. We see miracles every day in God's creation. I live in Montana, coined Big Sky Country. The sunrises and sunsets are miraculous and beautiful. The white glistening of a snowcapped mountain is almost mystifying. Open roads where golden wheat fields meet the horizon, stunning. Our landscape encompasses moonlit nights with millions of stars sparkling in the sky, falling stars, or trees swaying as if the hand of God gently grazes them. Miraculous is an understatement!

My Memories

My husband had a growth next to his ear, and the surgeon warned us that removing it could cause paralysis to that side of Dave's face and mouth or drooping and sagging if the nerves were accidently severed. We prayed and everyone we knew prayed for us. After the surgery, the surgeon said the growth was *almost gone* and it was an easy removal with no complications. Shaking his head, he said, "It must have been a miracle."

When people try to tell me God doesn't perform miracles today, I remember one story after another to tell them. Doctors told me I would *never* have children, but to my grateful surprise and the doctors' wonderment, I easily became pregnant. My mother called my daughter Kim the "miracle baby."

When my miracle baby became my prodigal who wanted nothing to do with God or prayer, I prayed for six long years for God to change her heart. Today, she's a godly woman who speaks with me and shares her testimony and we give God all the glory. When Kim lost all hope of ever having children herself, my husband and I prayed and fasted for God to help her become a parent. Today, she's the mother of three beautiful children—one adopted and two biological. Oh, yeah! God's still in the miracle business.

Your Memories

What miracles and wonders have you seen God do in your life? Times when your Red Sea opened up in front of you in a way only God could do, and you walked through unscathed as the waters closed in over sins, or a past that held you captive, or a feared fate. When was the last time you praised God for delivering you safely into his loving arms?

Or maybe your miracle was an answer to a long-petitioned prayer request. You didn't see it as a miracle at the time, but how can you redefine it as a miracle today?

Ways to Remember God's Goodness— *Pictures*...

In the Bible, God often used word pictures to describe himself and help us remember him—a Vinedresser, Potter, Builder, Lion, Lamb,

Husband, Father, Teacher—and we were made in his image. Look in the mirror and see a reminder of a miracle—you.

Pictures are a great way to remember the attributes of God and his goodness in performing miracles and blessed experiences. My photographer friend Karen confirms, "As a photographer, I don't take your photo; I provide you with a memory."

If you're not accustomed to taking pictures, start now. They'll be a visual reminder of the wonders and miracles God's been up to in your life. Maybe a picture of the first house or car you thought you could never afford. Or the beauty of your wedding, when you doubted ever finding the right spouse. The baby picture of the child you didn't ever expect to have or expected to have problems, but that child is perfect and blesses your life tenfold.

Look back through your picture albums, boxes of pictures, or digital photos, and mentally frame each one as a memory of the wonders you have seen God do in your life. Pick one or two that especially remind you of the wonders of God and use them as wallpaper on your computer screen or cell phone, frame them for your desk, pin them to a bulletin board, post them on your Facebook timeline, share them on Instagram, or tape them to your bathroom mirror—put them in places you see every day.

Make a habit of taking pictures—you never know when God is going to perform the next wonder or miracle and show you a memorable moment. You don't want to miss the treasure.

Let's Pray

Lord, I know you're performing wonders and miracles around me every day. Help me recognize them as the miracles they are and capture them in my mind and in pictures. Remind me to ascribe all the glory to you. Help me not to become complacent about your magnificent, miraculous presence in my life and in the world. Amen.

Talk about It

1. Do you believe God still performs miracles today? Why or why not?

2. What miracle are you waiting and praying for expectantly?

3. Are you in awe of God or complacent? How would remembering and honoring God's previous wonders and miracles in your life help you through a current difficulty?

4. Take a group picture or group selfie to remember the wonders you will experience together in this group. If you're reading this book on your own, take a selfie holding this book.

Chapter Eight

Honoring His Purpose

For it is God who works in you to will and to act in order to fulfill his good purpose.

—Philippians 2:13

You were made for God, not vice versa, and life is about letting God use you for his purposes, not you using him for your own purpose.

—Rick Warren[1]

Bible Memories

When the Israelites were fleeing Egypt and came up against the Red Sea blocking their escape, they must have wondered if God was truly good. How could he free them from bondage only to block their escape with an immovable body of water? What was his purpose in that? But we know the end of the story—God's purpose was for the good of the people and for him to receive the honor and glory. The end of Psalm 77 honors God as the good shepherd of his flock:

> Your path led through the sea,
>   your way through the mighty waters,
>   though your footprints were not seen.

> You led your people like a flock
>> by the hand of Moses and Aaron. (Ps. 77:19–20)

While the Israelites didn't see God in physical form, he used Moses and Aaron as his earthly shepherds. The Jews have told the miraculous freedom story throughout the generations to remind their people, and *all* people, of God's power, protection, and purpose for those he loves so dearly.

Chris and Holly Remember God's Goodness

Chris and Holly have learned to watch God direct their married life. Even when they don't understand what God's up to, they take significant risks to follow his call and purpose.

In our twenty plus years of marriage, I [Chris] have learned God often starts new seasons of our life by talking to my wife Holly. Honestly, that's probably because he starts with me and I'm just not listening well enough.

For example, when we felt God's calling to Colorado, I was still working at Libby Glass and we were living in Texas. I was "kind of" looking for work in Colorado on the side. God told Holly it would be okay if I went ahead and quit my job. Long story short, I went from "no way" to "this is what I'm going to do" over a weekend spent with the Father.

So when Holly told me about her current vision for us moving back to Texas and me teaching classes at A&M, I immediately perked up my spiritual listening ears and began to look to see what God was doing and saying.

I thought about how for years I've wanted to either write a book or create a class for young engineers on lessons I've learned about how to relate to others in our work environments. I've seen young engineers irreparably damage their careers in their first few weeks at a company from making bad relational decisions. I think I can help.

Next, I thought of how Holly and I have felt called to begin teaching young marrieds in college Sunday school class again. Then I looked at how God had been reintroducing us to the demographic of today's college students through exchange students staying with us last year.

Finally, I thought of our son Noah's desire to go to A&M and how returning to Texas might facilitate that dream.

I look back at God's work in our past and see signposts pointing toward where he seems to be heading us in our future and it seems consistent. I don't know the timing of it all, but I trust God does and we want to honor his purpose and plans for our lives.

My Memories

For years, as I spoke and looked out at audiences of women, I would be thinking: *Statistics predict one in eight of these women will get breast cancer.* I pleaded with the Lord not to let me be the "one in eight." When it *was* me, I was shocked. Hadn't I been praying I wouldn't get this dreaded disease? How could God use me in ministry if I had cancer?

But like Chris wrote in his story, I had seen God fulfill his purpose in my life in the past, and I knew he had a purpose in my breast cancer, too. It's as if the Lord had been preparing me for this tragic event, and I heard him say, *How selfish of you to pray you wouldn't be the one in eight. Why not you?*

My thinking changed when I realized the purpose in my breast cancer was that I would write the book I wished had been available when I was going through the battle myself. "Surviving for a Purpose" is the first chapter in *Dear God, They Say It's Cancer.* Here's a quote from that chapter:

> My purpose in writing *Dear God, They Say It's Cancer* is to help you and me be more than women who do or do not "survive breast cancer," but instead, women who seek and find God's purpose in it. God never wastes a hurt. Nothing happens by accident in a believer's life. For each of us, God's plan and purpose will be different. I know my purpose is to share my God-given passion to raise the awareness of prevention and early detection of breast cancer, as well as help those on the breast cancer journey live a quality of life in the secure arms of the Lord.[2]

God's purpose for my breast cancer was for me to come alongside other breast cancer sisters and offer them hope and encouragement through a relationship with Jesus Christ.

Your Memories

God has a purpose for every believer—the events in our lives are not random. Do you know God's purpose for your life? That purpose can change during different seasons of life, but we should never lack purpose.

Can you remember a time when you felt your life didn't have meaning or purpose? Maybe it was before you accepted Jesus Christ as your Savior. Remembering the emptiness you felt without purpose can help you seek and discover God's purpose for you now. What might that purpose be?

Ways to Remember God's Goodness—
Learning from the Past .... ✐

In his story, Chris said God often spoke through his wife, Holly. I find God often speaks purpose into my life through my husband, Dave. I also notice that when God's trying to get my attention, God confirms his plans and purpose through varied avenues.

Read Chris and Holly's story again and list the ways Chris "perked up his spiritual listening ears" to what God was doing and saying. Next to each item on your list for Chris, write down a comparable way God has shown you his purpose for your life in the past.

How might God be speaking to you now about his purpose and plan for the circumstances currently in your life? How will looking at your list help you honor that purpose?

Let's Pray

Lord, I know you created me for a reason and I want to honor your purpose. Help me keep my spiritual antenna up and be willing to go where you lead and do what you ask. Thank you for guiding and leading me in the past. Now please show me the plans you have for me today, and give me the courage to take whatever risk or challenge this might entail. Help me be brave, obedient, and purposeful. Amen.

Talk about It

1. How does Jeremiah 29:11 assure you God has a good purpose for you?

> "For I know the plans I have for you," declares the LORD, "plans to prosper you and not to harm you, plans to give you hope and a future."

God's plans are much better and higher than my plans. He has my best in mind when all I can see is this moment.

2. Does 1 Corinthians 2:9 (NLT) fill you with excitement or dread? Explain.

> No eye has seen, no ear has heard, and no mind has imagined what God has prepared for those who love him.

Excitement bc. God is never finished when we are. I can't begin to imagine how He can and will work, He is ALmighty and infinitely Good.

3. The first line in Pastor Rick Warren's best seller *The Purpose Driven Life* states, "It's not about you."³ How might God's purpose for you involve doing good for others rather than focusing on your own achievements?

Serving people at my job and at home in humility to please my Father, whether anyone notices or not.

4. If you're not living a purpose driven life, what would it take to accomplish that goal?

Daily surrendering my decisions, attitude to my Lord for Him to use me for His eternal purposes.

SECTION THREE

PRAISING GOD

*I will praise the L*ORD *at all times.*
I will constantly speak his praises.

—Psalm 34:1 NLT

I look back at so much of my life and see how God has used it in
spite of me; how He has accepted my imperfection; how He has
woven people in and out of my life at the perfect times; how He has
blessed me beyond my wildest dreams; and how He has allowed
me to be in His presence while He worked miracles. My mind
doesn't fathom that kind of love and dedication, but my heart does.
That, to me, is awe-inspiring and completely humbling.

—Heidi Paulson[1]

God is worthy of our praise. Praising him in *all* circumstances reminds us of his abounding goodness, even during difficult seasons. Heidi Paulson wrote the opening quote even after her police officer husband had been in two tragic and crippling motorcycle accidents. Still, she praised God.

Numerous verses prompt us to live in an attitude of praise. In the Bible, we repeatedly see desperate people seeking God and praying in faith; he meets their need, and they often praise him in song. For the purposes of this section, we'll look at the Book of Psalms and 1 Chronicles 16 for ways to incorporate the ministry of praise into our daily life.

Chapter Nine

Praising His Creation

Be glad; rejoice forever in my creation!

—Isaiah 65:18a NLT

I try to see and praise the miraculous beauty of God's creation every day.

—Heidi Williams

Bible Memories

God helped King David defeat the Philistines and successfully move the ark of the Lord back to Jerusalem. There was a great praise celebration: "So all Israel brought up the ark of the covenant of the LORD with shouts, with the sounding of rams' horns and trumpets, and of cymbals, and the playing of lyres and harps" (1 Chron. 15:28). Then David told the Levites that "they were to play the lyres and harps, Asaph was to sound the cymbals, and Benaiah and Jahaziel the priests were to blow the trumpets regularly before the ark of the covenant of God" (1 Chron. 16:5b–6).

Blowing the trumpets was God's ordinance before going into battle and at celebrations. "Also at your times of rejoicing—your appointed festivals and New Moon feasts—you are to sound the trumpets over your burnt offerings and fellowship offerings, and they will be a memorial for you before your God. I am the LORD your God" (Num. 10:10).

Then David had Asaph write a psalm of thanksgiving to the Lord, not just for the current victory, but in remembrance of all the marvelous deeds, wonders, and miracles the Lord had done for his people.

That day David first appointed Asaph and his associates to give praise to the LORD in this manner:

Give praise to the LORD, proclaim his name;
    make known among the nations what he has done.
Sing to him, sing praise to him;
    tell of all his wonderful acts.
Glory in his holy name;
    let the hearts of those who seek the LORD rejoice.
Look to the LORD and his strength;
    seek his face always.

Remember the wonders he has done,
    his miracles, and the judgments he pronounced,
you his servants, the descendants of Israel,
    his chosen ones, the children of Jacob.
He is the LORD our God;
    his judgments are in all the earth.
(1 Chron. 16:7–14)

David used this time of rejoicing to revisit God's goodness throughout the generations. In verse 15, David reminds them, "He [God] remembers his covenant forever, the promise he made, for a thousand generations." Then, in verses 16–23, David lists the promises of God. Next, David affirms something only God can claim—"In the beginning God created the heavens and the earth" (Gen. 1:1).

> For great is the LORD and most worthy of praise;
> > he is to be feared above all gods.
> For all the gods of the nations are idols,
> > but the LORD made the heavens.
> Splendor and majesty are before him;
> > strength and joy are in his dwelling place.
> (1 Chron. 16:25–27)

And God has made a covenant and promise with his creation—earth and us—that never again will he destroy the earth like he did in the era of Noah and the flood. Knowing how our world has deteriorated since then—and many liken our current culture to the "days of Noah"—I'm sure it takes great restraint for God not to be done with us. That's why every time I see a rainbow, I pray, "Praise you Lord for your goodness. Thank you for your promises and your blessings." Won't you join me in praise when you see a rainbow? Because the Lord has promised us in Genesis 9:13–16:

> I have set my rainbow in the clouds, and it will be
> the sign of the covenant between me and the earth.
> Whenever I bring clouds over the earth and the rainbow
> appears in the clouds, I will remember my covenant
> between me and you and all living creatures of every
> kind. Never again will the waters become a flood to
> destroy all life. Whenever the rainbow appears in the
> clouds, I will see it and remember the everlasting cov-
> enant between God and all living creatures of every
> kind on the earth.

The secular world that rejects God is the same world that God *spoke* into creation and commits to sustain. Never lose sense of the supremacy and majesty of our great and awesome God. Never forget that the same all-powerful God who created an intricate universe is the same God who created you!

Karen O'Conner Remembers God's Goodness

There's nothing like a visual of God's miraculous creation to help us remember God's goodness in the midst of our personal storms. Karen O'Conner was feeling discouraged and defeated until someone challenged her to appreciate the wonders of God's hidden treasures.

Everywhere I looked was trash. Finances. Career. Marriage. Family relationships. Nothing worked anymore.

To get away from the pain and confusion—at least for a day—I ran off to the mountains with some hiking friends. A good workout was just what I needed to gain some perspective.

After the first hour on the trail, I could barely stand up. The rough patch of road went up and down like a rollercoaster and we lost ground almost as quickly as we gained it. "Not sure I can go on," I shouted. Others echoed my viewpoint.

Hal, one of the stronger hikers, charged ahead and then turned and shouted, "Come on. The *real* treasure is up here. You've got to see this view." His enthusiasm caught my attention. I plowed ahead.

What a sight it was. Treasures as far as the eye could see. Beautiful peaks poked above the clouds, tall trees and flowering shrubs dotted the hillsides, and small lakes and streams sparkled in the sun.

To think I almost missed these gifts—all because I was so weary and heavy-laden. I came home a different person—ready to face my problems with a new and higher point of view. Could what I saw as trash, God see as buried treasure? I couldn't wait to find out. I learned in a fresh way that *God is good—all the time.*

My Memories

My husband and I live in a beautiful rural mountain environment in Idaho. A hidden treasure tucked away in the mountains and forest with a river running through town, deer and elk lounging in our yard, and squirrels scurrying up trees. Every morning as I open the blinds, I stand in wonderment and awe at the breathtaking, magnificent view awaiting me. Only God could create something as beautiful as nature.

Before moving to Idaho, we lived on a street appropriately named Sunset Lane, not far from the beach in Southern California, with the ocean and its pounding surf and spectacular sunsets. At dusk, I would look out our picture windows and marvel at the sunsets God brilliantly painted across the horizon—each one unique and spectacular. Today, a majestic forest surrounds our home and the trees block my view of sunsets. I miss them, but I have great memories of twenty-four years of sunsets on Sunset Lane. They never grew old.

Now I experience a different reminder of God's glorious creation. As I write this, I'm reminded of Joyce Kilmer's poem "Trees," and her last line, "But only God can make a tree."

Your Memories

Wherever you live, God's creation surrounds you because he created *everything*. Even if you live in the city, you see the moon, sun, stars, sky, flowers, grass—God's creation is everywhere.

What is your earliest memory of experiencing creation? Maybe rolling in the grass or in a pile of leaves, making mud pies, playing in a sandbox, swimming in a lake, planting seeds and watching them grow, or seeing a rainbow for the first time . . . Perhaps you were too young to acknowledge God as the Creator of everything, but can you remember the joy and pleasure you experienced enjoying his creation?

If you're able, take a walk outside and breathe in fresh air. Lie down in the grass or a hammock; sit in a swing or lawn chair. Pick up a handful of dirt and smell the earth, or grab a glove full of snow and make a snowball or snowman. Take a walk or jog and talk to God. If you can't go outside, gaze out the window and enjoy the sunshine or the cloud formations or the stars in the galaxy.

Inside, or outside, let your mind wander back to those early days of childhood and write here your first creation memory.

Ways to Remember God's Goodness—
Praise and Worship Music .... ✒

In 1 Chronicles 16:7–14, David told the people to sing praises to God and had Asaph write a psalm, which is also a song. Singing praise and worship songs is a joyful way to remember God's miraculous creation. When you sing in church, think about the words of the songs. Many songs praise the wonders of God's majesty and creation. And, by the way, don't be late for church. You don't want to miss the worship time that prepares your heart for the pastor's message.

Surround yourself with praise music on your radio, electronic device, computer, TV, or Internet station. Play praise music in your home and in the car. Listen to praise songs while you exercise or relax. Listen to the songwriter's lyrics. Sing along. If you play a musical instrument, accompany the song. Could God be asking you to play in the praise band at church? Sing with the worship team?

When you're going through a tough time and need a reminder of God's faithfulness and goodness, sing or listen to one of your favorite praise songs. Chances are the author of the song was going through something similar when he or she penned the lyrics. Write some of the words from the praise songs that especially speak to you.

Let's Pray

Lord, it's so easy to take for granted the majesty and wonder of the heavens and earth you created. Help me be more aware of the beauty surrounding me and nudge me to remind others to notice your creative artwork. When I see a rainbow, remind me to praise you. I don't always see creation as the miracle it surely is, and I often don't recognize your hand in my daily activities. Give me eyes to see and a mouth to sing and tell others of your wondrous ways and your magnificent creation. Amen.

Talk about It

1. What praise song reminds you most of God's creation?

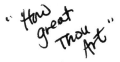

2. How does singing or playing praise and worship music remind you of God's goodness?

It directs my thoughts upward

3. What is your favorite part of nature? Explain why.

Pretty flowers & Views, green grass, lakes & ocean, birds, butterflies, sounds of singing birds, waterfalls. They are peaceful & calming

4. Look out the window and describe what you see. How does your perspective of your surroundings change when you think of them as God's marvelous creation?

I see the breeze & the birds singing & happily chirping, The flowers are blooming brightly, the sky is a lovely blue.

Chapter Ten

Praising
His Faithfulness

It is good to praise the LORD
and make music to your name, O Most High,
proclaiming your love in the morning
and your faithfulness at night,
to the music of the ten-stringed lyre
and the melody of the harp.
—Psalm 92:1–3

God's past faithfulness helps us trust him in the future.
—Kathy Howard

Bible Memories

When God closed the Red Sea over the Egyptian army after the Israelites had crossed through on dry ground and were safe on shore, Moses and the Israelites celebrated their freedom by singing a praise song known as the "Song to Yahweh" or "Song of Moses" (Exod. 15:1–21). Moses knew that commemorating this miracle in a song would help the people remember the faithfulness and goodness of their great Rescuer.

Then Miriam the prophet, Aaron's sister, took a
tambourine and led all the women as they played their
tambourines and danced. And Miriam sang this song:

"Sing to the LORD,
for he has triumphed gloriously;
he has hurled both horse and rider
into the sea." (Exod. 15:20–21 NLT)

David's Psalm of Thanksgiving in 1 Chronicles 16:15–24 reminds
the people of God's faithfulness to their ancestors. While the previous generations often forgot their covenant to God, God remembers his covenants to his people "forever." God is faithful, and
he expects us to be faithful in praising and thanking him for his
goodness to us and to all generations.

He remembers his covenant forever,
the promise he made, for a thousand generations,
the covenant he made with Abraham,
the oath he swore to Isaac.
He confirmed it to Jacob as a decree,
to Israel as an everlasting covenant:
"To you I will give the land of Canaan
as the portion you will inherit."

When they were but few in number,
few indeed, and strangers in it,
they wandered from nation to nation,
from one kingdom to another.
He allowed no one to oppress them;
for their sake he rebuked kings:
"Do not touch my anointed ones;
do my prophets no harm."

Sing to the LORD, all the earth;
  proclaim his salvation day after day.
Declare his glory among the nations,
  his marvelous deeds among all peoples.

The Israelites inherited the land of Canaan as God had promised,
and he protected them as long as they obeyed him. A crucial ele-
ment of any promise or covenant is that the recipient accepts the
ensuing *stipulations* and *blessings*. God told the Israelites to go
in and possess *all* of the land he was giving them, but because of
unbelief, indifference, fear, and forgetfulness, they seldom enjoyed
the full extent of God's gifts to them.

[handwritten margin note: Where is my unbelief & fear causing me not to enjoy God to the fullest extent possible]

Kathy Collard Miller Remembers God's Goodness

Kathy Collard Miller shares a vulnerable moment with the Lord
when praising him reminded her of God's faithfulness in the past
as encouragement for the moment.

> I was so angry: *Why can't my husband Larry reach out to
> our son and see Mark needs encouragement?* Tears welled
> in my eyes. My heart was heavy with worry about what
> would happen to Mark if this toxic relationship contin-
> ued. The night's darkness mirrored my fear of the future.
> I pounded on the steering wheel, "God, change Larry!"
>   *Praise me!*
>   "Praise you?" I retorted. "What good will that do?
> Praising you means I focus on who you are and give you
> glory when I don't like what you're doing." Determined
> to be angry and fearful, I tried to resist the nudges to
> think on God's past faithfulness. This was a new prob-
> lem and I needed help *right now*.

Praise released
God's power

The Holy Spirit persisted. I reviewed in my mind the glorifications of God delivering me from being a child abuser. He had healed our marriage on the brink of divorce and allowed our story to encourage others. Remembering God's past sovereignty and faithfulness became a light at the end of a dark tunnel.

Praise me, reverberated through my brain again.

My heart didn't want to go there, but God was prompting me with the power to praise him. I feebly mumbled, "I praise you, God." Again, with a little more conviction, "Okay, God, I *do* praise you."

Then I began singing my praise. Somehow, that sounded more authentic. My voice became stronger with more conviction: "Okay, Lord, I release my anger and my need to control. I praise you for your faithfulness." My heart softened and joy stirred my heart to trust God in whatever way he chose—even if it was nothing.

Arriving home, I got ready for bed with praise songs echoing in my mind. I tried not to wake Larry, but he said in a sleepy voice, "Kath, what do you think about me asking Mark if he wants to learn to play golf? Then he could join me on the course. I've been trying to think of something we could do together and that seems like a good choice."

Oh, Lord, you are faithful . . . I'm so sorry I tried to take control . . . again. Tearfully, I whispered, "Yeah, honey, I think that's a great idea."

My Memories

I am a three-time breast cancer survivor. As I mentioned earlier, I found purpose in my first diagnosis by writing a book for other breast cancer sisters. But with the second and third diagnoses, I was troubled. Statistics said that with the treatment I had for the first round of cancer, there was only a one-percent chance of it returning. Yet here I was with two recurrences. I questioned how God could let this happen, when I was so busy writing and speaking for him.

My comfort came from finding ways to sing his praises—not for having breast cancer, but for his faithfulness to see me through three occurrences. Praise for everyone who rallied to help and support me each time. For mammograms that detected my cancer early. For a supportive and loving husband. For opportunities to witness during surgeries and treatment. For the book I wrote that now was blessing me as well as others. For skillful doctors. For second opinions. For a body that bounced back each time. Praising God for his past faithfulness gave me the courage and peace to endure each new recurrence.

Now when I go for my frequent checkups, I praise him loudly for healing me to this point and give him all the glory and praise when the tests show no new cancer. I pray I won't have a fourth time, but still I will praise him.

Your Memories

You might associate praise with thanking God for a joyous circumstance, but how often do you praise him in the midst of a troubling situation? The answer lies in whether you believe with your whole heart that God is good . . . all the time. Do you trust God will be faithful to make a way where there seems to be no way, and that he always has a specific plan and purpose for you? Past memories of God's faithfulness bolstered Kathy Collard Miller to praise God even when she didn't feel like praising him. She wasn't happy; she was mad. Praise changed her heart and her attitude.

God is faithful to fulfill his promises to all generations, but even when the Israelites moved into the Promised Land, they still had to overcome obstacles in possessing the land. Think back to a time when you could see God's faithfulness even though things weren't going like you expected or wanted. If you haven't already acknowledged God in the midst of that circumstance, or you didn't praise him regardless of the outcome, give him praise right now. Notice how it changes your attitude toward the situation.

Today, I do praise you, my Good, Good Father. This world is a sad place b/c. of Sin. My loved ones are suffering b/c of Sin's grip in addictions, illnesses, and Satan's deceit. I praise you that you are going to right all wrongs and make everything beautiful in your time.

Ways to Remember God's Goodness—
Singing Scripture ....

If you're going through a difficult season, or angry with God, still praise him with all the strength and energy you can muster. Remember his past faithfulness so you can trust his current faithfulness. Soon, like Kathy, you might find yourself singing a praise song or maybe singing Scripture like the Israelites and David did. Christian songwriters get their inspiration for songs from life experiences and the Scriptures, especially the Psalms. Reading through the Book of Psalms is always helpful during trying times.

Singing is also a great way to memorize Scripture. For example, you probably recognize these lyrics:

- Our Father which art in heaven . . . from Matthew 6:9–13 (KJV).
- You are worthy, our Lord and God, to receive glory and honor and power . . . from Revelation 4:11.
- Wonderful Counselor, Mighty God, Everlasting Father, Prince of Peace . . . from Isaiah 9:6.

- Let everything that has breath praise the LORD . . . from Psalm 150:6.

You know more Scripture than you think you do! Google "Scripture in song," and you'll find many options to download, or look for CDs to help you learn Scripture to have ready in your heart to sing and praise the Lord for his faithfulness.

You've heard the phrase, "He can't stop singing her praises." He isn't literally singing, but he's talking nonstop about all her wonderful, amazing qualities. So even if you don't sing, let others say of you, "They can't stop singing God's praises."

Let's Pray

Lord, thank you for your limitless faithfulness to me . . . even when I'm not faithful to give you the credit and praise you deserve. Remind me moment by moment of the things I should be thankful for and help me eliminate fear, anxiety, anger, and any control issues. In difficult times, refresh my memory with the many ways you have shown your faithfulness to me in the past. Help me learn your Scriptures and meditate on their meaning. I'll sing your praises, Lord, all day long! Amen.

Talk about It

1. Why is it so difficult to praise God when things aren't going our way or we're angry? We are fearful and don't want to walk through our pain, we want God to fix our problems.

2. God is always faithful to his people:

He will keep you strong to the end so that you will be free from all blame on the day when our Lord Jesus Christ returns. God will do this, for he is faithful to do

what he says, and he has invited you into partnership
with his Son, Jesus Christ our Lord. (1 Cor. 1:8–9 NLT)

What is our part of God's promise? As a Christian, how do you
react to that promise?

Partner with Jesus in being faithful to God

3. What does *faithful* mean to you?

*Loyal, committed, obedient, persistent
integrity, wholeheartedly His*

4. Why do we forget to "sing God's praises" and thank him for
his faithfulness?

*We (I)
are too
preoccupied
with ourselves
and our being
"needs"
met that
we forget the One.
who can
have and help us
most.*

Chapter Eleven

Praising His Compassion

Let my whole being bless the LORD
and never forget all his good deeds:
how God forgives all your sins,
heals all your sickness,
saves your life from the pit,
crowns you with faithful love and compassion

—Psalm 103:2–4 CEB

Not only had God given me new body parts,
He'd also given me a whole new perspective.
I'd never take it for granted. It was all too good.

—Ema McKinley[1]

[Handwritten note: Lord, I thank you for the beauty of this day — You are the creator of it and your Majesty is worthy of my praise. Thank you that you reign eternal and one day the Heavens will hold you and we will behold your glory, never to be apart from you again — O glorious day.]

Bible Memories

Psalms are spiritual songs and prayers of praise for God's goodness, greatness, love, and compassion—what you feel when someone else is hurting. God is compassionate and felt the pain of his people, but they seldom felt the pain they caused him. God loved the Israelites, but Moses lamented, "You have been rebellious against the LORD ever since I have known you" (Deut. 9:24). Still, God would never forsake them, even as they forsook him. In spite of their blatant disobedience and continuous grumbling, God had compassion for his people: "He will not leave you, destroy you, or forget the covenant with your fathers that He swore to them by oath, because the LORD your God is a compassionate God" (Deut. 4:31 HCSB).

Psalm 111:1–5 reminds us how, and why, we praise God in a way that acknowledges his love and compassion for us:

Praise the LORD.

I will extol the LORD with all my heart
    in the council of the upright and in the assembly.

Great are the works of the LORD;
    they are pondered by all who delight in them.
Glorious and majestic are his deeds,
    and his righteousness endures forever.
He has caused his wonders to be remembered;
    the LORD is gracious and compassionate.
He provides food for those who fear him;
    he remembers his covenant forever.

Today, God uses the followers of Jesus Christ to be his hands and feet in showing tangible love and compassion to others in need of help. He blesses all who serve in his name and for his purpose.

Then the King will say to those on his right, "Come, you who are blessed by my Father; take your inheritance, the kingdom prepared for you since the creation of the world. For I was hungry and you gave me something to eat, I was thirsty and you gave me something to drink, I was a stranger and you invited me in, I needed clothes and you clothed me, I was sick and you looked after me, I was in prison and you came to visit me."

Then the righteous will answer him, "Lord, when did we see you hungry and feed you, or thirsty and give you something to drink? When did we see you a stranger and invite you in, or needing clothes and clothe you? When did we see you sick or in prison and go to visit you?"

The King will reply, "Truly I tell you, whatever you did for one of the least of these brothers and sisters of mine, you did for me." (Matt. 25:34–40)

Remember to praise God for lavishing his kindness and compassion on you, but praise him even more for using you to lavish his kindness and compassion on someone else.

Dawn Wilson Remembers God's Goodness

Forty years later, Dawn still remembers the transforming experience of God lavishing his kindness and compassion on her through one of his humble earthly servants.

At twenty-one, I jumped at the opportunity to sing and serve with Life Action Ministries, a national revival ministry, and travel throughout the United States. I couldn't believe God had called me to such a powerful ministry. Still, I struggled with the ten-dollar allotment for personal needs.

Soon I needed the basics like toothpaste, hair spray, deodorant, feminine supplies, nylons, makeup, breath mints, and thank you notes for the hosts where I stayed each week. I became so desperate I even considered leaving the team.

I cried out to God, "Didn't you call me here? You know I don't have these things. I've watched you provide *spiritually* for people in the churches. Won't you please provide *practically* for me?"

The next week, another team member and I stayed with an elderly woman. Her house from the outside looked small and downtrodden: *the lady must be poor and we'll have a rough week.* I was pleasantly surprised to find her home comfortable and cheerful inside. She offered us a glass of cool water and led us to the room where we would stay for the week.

I burst into tears. On each bed was a welcome gift basket. *Everything* I needed and prayed for was in that basket—and not in small sample sizes! This dear, sweet, godly woman had thought of everything—the personal supplies, thank you notes, chocolates, and an envelope with twenty dollars for "whatever else you need."

Humbly, I confessed my lack of faith: "Oh, Father God, you are so good to me. Thank you for your goodness. Your faithfulness. Your compassion." Then I ran to tell the sweet lady about my prayer request to God.

I've long since forgotten her name, but never her kindness. I've learned to place my confidence in God for all things, not just my daily needs. I still remember the "faithfulness basket" as the foundation of my understanding that God is compassionate and faithful to provide for his beloved children.

My Memories

I've been the recipient on more than one occasion of God's kindness and compassion extended through human hands. Following surgeries, during breast cancer treatments, and after I broke my foot, the Saddleback Church Meals Ministry brought complete meals to us. What a blessing to open the front door and see a kind, compassionate, smiling servant of God standing on the porch with baskets and plates of food.

Now that we've moved to Idaho, several women from our new church have brought Dave and me dinners during my book deadlines so I wouldn't have to stop writing to cook. In all my years of writing and deadlines, this is a first! We praise God for these precious women with servant hearts who recognize a genuine need and graciously let God use them to lavish his kindness and compassion on us.

I wish I could say I always remember to do the same when I hear of an illness, surgery, or someone trying to accomplish an overwhelming task. I'm faithful to pray, but everyone needs a human extension of God's compassion, and we need to praise God for those who remember to be his compassionate earthly servants.

Your Memories

Can you remember a time when God used earthly servants to extend his compassion to you in a tangible way? You probably thanked his servants, but did you stop and praise him for sending them?

Or maybe you were like the sweet woman in Dawn's story or the women who brought Dave and me meals, and you let God use you to compassionately, maybe even sacrificially, meet someone else's needs. Did you praise God for using you as his servant?

Reflect on how it feels to *receive* service and *extend* service. If you haven't given God the praise—either way—do so here.

Ways to Remember God's Goodness—
Service .... ⌇

It's easy to receive service; it's work to serve. A memorable way to remember God's goodness is to be a source of goodness and compassion to others. In Dawn's story, the elderly woman was living a frugal lifestyle, yet she opened her home to the girls and spent her own money to provide them with a gift basket and extra money. When Dawn told her that she was an answer to prayer, you know the woman never forgot how God used her as his earthly servant.

If you're serving in a ministry or volunteer organization, your service is helping others. Remember their faces, words of thanks, and appreciation. Consider that you are representing God's compassion for those people's needs. Let the recipients know the glory goes to God with a simple, "God loves you." Or, "I'm serving God when I serve you." You'll remain humble and remember *all* good gifts come from God, and they'll remember that, too.

If you're not serving in a ministry or volunteer capacity, ask God to show you an opportunity that fits your gifts and abilities. If time is an issue, how about praying for one of the young people in the youth ministry at church—stand in the gap for him or her. Every January, our church passes out laminated bookmarks with a picture of each child in the children's ministry, and the congregation takes a bookmark and prays for that child during the year.

Who needs your help today? What could you do to make his or her life easier? Do it. I guarantee serving will draw you closer to God, and you'll never forget the experience.

Let's Pray

God, you are so compassionate, kind, and good. Please help me develop those virtues and remind me to use them lavishly to your glory. Thank you for your loving compassion every day, even when I'm undeserving. Show me where you would have me serve you. I praise you, Lord, for caring about me as you do. Amen.

Talk about It

1. Discuss how to apply in today's world Matthew 25:34–40 from the Bible Memories section.

2. How would you describe God's compassion?

Abundant   personal
timely   sweet

3. Read this story from Heidi Williams and then discuss what you would have done. How was Heidi's compassion a witness?

> I was driving home from work after a twelve-hour work-day, exhausted, hungry, thirsty, and wanting to get home. Pulling up to a stoplight, I noticed an unkempt old man with long, dirty hair and missing teeth carrying the sign "Vietnam Vet, anything helps, God Bless you." His shopping cart was full of "treasures."
>
> As I made eye contact and smiled, the Lord whispered, *He's hungry too.* I thought, *Oh, Lord, please not tonight. I'm so tired and I just want to go home.* The Lord continued to nudge, so I pulled into a fast-food restaurant and bought food. Walking up to the man, I reached out my hand to grab his and noticed it was filthy, his

nose was dripping, and he was wearing a portable cath-eter. *I'm probably going to get sick. Do I really have to do this?* I handed him the food and made small talk. His name was Gene and he had a trailer. His arthritis was acting up badly.

When I got home, my sister texted, "Were you wit-nessing to that old grandpa?" She had driven by while I was on the street corner with him.

4. Would you consider yourself a compassionate person? Why or why not?

Chapter Twelve

Praising
His Provision

I will bless her with abundant provisions;
her poor I will satisfy with food.

—Psalm 132:15

God's great and precious promises are like a forgotten storehouse
containing priceless goods.

—Chris Tiegreen[1]

Bible Memories

In Psalm 78, the psalmist Asaph retells the story of the Jewish nation from the time of slavery in Egypt to the reign of King David. The opening verses of this psalm recall their freedom journey. Then, in verses 17–20, Asaph recounts their demands, doubts, and rebellion:

But they continued to sin against him,
    rebelling in the wilderness against the Most High.
They willfully put God to the test
    by demanding the food they craved.
They spoke against God;
    they said, "Can God really
      spread a table in the wilderness?
True, he struck the rock,

> and water gushed out,
>   streams flowed abundantly,
> but can he also give us bread?
>   Can he supply meat for his people?"

God probably would have sustained them without food; after all, their clothes never wore out and their feet didn't swell with all the walking they did for forty years in the wilderness (Deut. 8:4). In spite of their ungrateful and mocking attitude, God gave them food: "Yet he gave a command to the skies above and opened the doors of the heavens; he rained down manna for the people to eat, he gave them the grain of heaven. Human beings ate the bread of angels; he sent them all the food they could eat" (Ps. 78:23–25).

Surely they would remember God's provision and love for them now, but enough was never enough.

> In spite of all this, they kept on sinning;
>   in spite of his wonders, they did not believe.
> So he ended their days in futility
>   and their years in terror.
> Whenever God slew them, they would seek him;
>   they eagerly turned to him again.
> They remembered that God was their Rock,
>   that God Most High was their Redeemer.
> But then they would flatter him with their mouths,
>   lying to him with their tongues;
> their hearts were not loyal to him,
>   they were not faithful to his covenant. (Ps. 78:32–37)

> Again and again they put God to the test;
>   they vexed the Holy One of Israel.
> They did not remember his power—
>   the day he redeemed them from the oppressor,

the day he displayed his signs in Egypt,
   his wonders in the region of Zoan. (Ps. 78:41–43)

The Israelites' ingratitude for God's goodness to them eventually eroded their relationship with God. How heartbroken God must have been with their misremembering and ongoing disrespect. How heartbroken God must be when we misremember and disrespect him.

Penelope Carlevato Remembers God's Goodness

Penelope had forgotten the following incident, until I asked her if she ever forgot God's goodness. Remembering and telling this story reminded her of God's faithful provision.

Hard times hit our family. My husband had quit a great job he loved to invest in what turned out to be a fraudulent company. We were so sure of the business venture, we became overconfident and prideful. Now we had no money, a big mortgage, three children, and the immediate problem: no food.

We were living in a lovely new home, had a shiny new car in the driveway, and looked like we were living the American dream. We were churchgoers but had begun wondering about this "God thing." Was one hour on Sunday enough?

We had met a couple who were new Christians and they kept nagging us to come with them to their fabulous church. Our new friends encouraged us to read our Bibles and pray. What did we have to lose?

While my husband was looking for work, I was babysitting a little boy for our neighbor who was a flight attendant. She would be coming to pick up her little guy about six o'clock, and I felt bad we didn't have anything to give him to eat. I wasn't even sure what I would do for *our* dinner. I remember sitting at the table with my husband talking to God, "Where will we get food for tonight? The cupboards are bare. God, what do we do?"

The little boy's mother arrived on time and came into the house with her arms full of packages in tinfoil. "Hope I don't offend you," she said, "but there were so many extra dinners left over on the flight, I just couldn't stand to see them thrown away."

We dined on First Class meals that night and the next. God didn't let us down. Even though we barely knew how to pray, God provided for us. Our story is such a good reminder of God's provision over the years.

My Memories

When I married my husband Dave, after being a single parent for seventeen years—the sole provider for my daughter and myself—I was ecstatic to have the blessing of a godly husband who was also an excellent provider. We both had great-paying careers and Dave had terrific benefits. After three years, I quit my job to go into full-time lay ministry starting the Woman to Woman Mentoring Ministry at Saddleback Church, and three months later, Dave went through the first of three job losses.

We were without benefits and he was unemployed for eighteen months. I had just started writing resources to help other churches start the Woman to Woman Mentoring Ministry, so neither of us was working. Our family and friends loudly vocalized they thought I should go back to work. Dave would respond, "Janet *is* working. She's about the Lord's work."

About His Work Ministries, my writing and speaking ministry, evolved from that difficult time. God saw us through and we always had just enough to get by. While the ministry flourished and we stayed faithful to God's "feed my sheep" ministry call, he provided for our needs.

So with Dave's next two layoffs and eventual early medical retirement, we weren't fearful because we remembered how God provided in the past, and we knew if we trusted him, continued serving him, and lived by his guidelines for our lives, we would be fine. We were, and we still are. You've heard it said where God guides, he provides. He surely has with us . . . and he will for you, too.

Your Memories

Everyone faces challenging times when we wonder if God will meet our needs. What is your memory of one of those times . . . maybe in the family you grew up in or as a starving college student or a struggling single mom? Have you had a frustrating career choice or a financial or job loss? Or maybe not so long ago—today in the doctor's office, the grocery store, at work, or in your family? What do you remember about getting through that difficult period or moment? Did you see God providing for your immediate needs? If you didn't recognize him at the time, can you look back and see how God's provision and love sustained you? Praise him for being your faithful Provider.

Ways to Remember God's Goodness—
Attending Church and Joining a Small Group.. ✒

Attending church regularly is essential to sustaining our faith, but we need to be *participants*, not *spectators*. Church is where we fellowship with other believers who encourage us as we encourage them. God uses the pastor's sermons to help us grow and mature in our faith.

Take your Bible to church, even if they put the Scriptures up on a screen or have them in a handout. Your Bible is your personal lifeline to God. You need to interact with it, highlight it, make notes, and look up the Scriptures so you can find them readily later. If your Bible is on a tablet, iPad, or cell phone, turn the sound off, look up the Scriptures on your electronic Bible, and take notes there. Not taking your Bible to church is like trying to drive a car without a steering wheel—when you try to advance forward, you crash!

Small groups, Bible studies, or life groups are an extension of church into your daily life. Participating in a group study provides the opportunity to expand on what you learn on Sundays, mature spiritually, and apply your faith. Others pray for your needs and you pray for their requests. Just as Penelope said in her story, going to church once a week on Sunday isn't enough. The Christian life is a way of life lived out in community with other believers.

If you've been an *attender* at church, consider becoming an *active member*. If you're not part of a small group or Bible study, find one to join. God doesn't want you to be a Lone Ranger Christian.

Let's Pray

Lord, you know how anxious and fearful I become over insufficient funds or the threat of loss of material possessions. My natural tendency is to try to remedy the situation myself. Lord, help me remember to pray first and ask for your help and provision, and then trust you'll take care of all my needs. Maybe not my wants, but you know best the necessities. I give you all the glory and praise for being my benevolent Provider. Amen.

Talk about It

1. Describe a time when you received a needed and specific provision. How did you react? Did you see God or a person as the provider? *New job & no money for food when God provided cash in my box along w/. bags of food & canned goods in one day! ☺ (Soccer shoes ☺) — jobs to provide needed $*

2. Why do we often forget God is our "Rock" and Provider? *Coming often. We try to be too self sufficient*

3. Tell a story of God using you as the source of his provision for someone else. *-Giving food & clothes to others - Compassion Kids*

4. Which of the Ways to Remember God's Goodness from previous chapters have you tried? How are they helping you remember God's goodness? *Using scripture*

Chapter Thirteen

Praising His Goodness

May the peoples praise you, God;
may all the peoples praise you.

—Psalm 67:3

The Psalmists in telling everyone to praise God are doing what all
men do when they speak of what they care about.

—C. S. Lewis[1]

Bible Memories

The following verses conclude David's Psalm of Thanksgiving in 1 Chronicles 16:8–36. Some Bible translations call this David's Song of Praise. The foundation of praise is ascribing to God his attributes and goodness in a way others hear and recognize. We praise God publically by praying, singing, writing, verbalizing, and sharing our faith. We also can enjoy quiet moments alone with God praising him privately, which displays publically in our smile, joy, and peace.

You'll notice that in the closing of David's praise song, he uses both "praise" and "give thanks." Giving thanks usually is for something we have received from God or for what he has done for us—somehow we've benefited—me-centered prayers. Praise focuses on God's character and goodness—who he is, not what he does—God-centered prayers.

> Give thanks to the LORD, for he is good;
> his love endures forever.
> Cry out, "Save us, God our Savior;
> gather us and deliver us from the nations,
> that we may give thanks to your holy name,
> and glory in your praise."
> Praise be to the LORD, the God of Israel,
> from everlasting to everlasting.
>
> Then all the people said "Amen" and "Praise the LORD."
> (1 Chron. 16:34–36)

The key to sincere praise is to live as if you believe God is good and worthy of your praise—not just saying the right words during worship and then returning to a world-centered life after the final amen. Praise God by letting your life be a witness to the goodness of God as you declare with the psalmist:

> "As for me, I will always have hope;
> I will praise you more and more." (Ps. 71:14)

Becky Harling Remembers God's Goodness

Becky Harling, author of *The 30-Day Praise Challenge*, is passionate about the blessings of praising God's goodness every day.

> I love that I can expect God to come close. He isn't distant, aloof, or emotionally cold. When I have times of praise in the early morning darkness, he comes close. His Spirit awakens my heart to more of his presence. I've been on this "praise journey," enjoying at least twenty minutes of praise each morning, since my mentor first gave me the praise challenge when I had breast cancer, and other areas of my life were falling apart.

Most mornings, I praise God on my knees in my office with headphones on listening to praise music and allowing the music to prompt my praise. Honestly, it has changed my life! As I became intentional about praising God, I experienced his presence as never before.

I spend *time* praising God. I praise him when I need wisdom, hope, or words for a manuscript. When I need healing—physical or emotional. I have come to realize I can do nothing without worshipping and praising him.

Our lives have heavy burdens—but when we praise God above the difficulties—God's presence comes close and he moves in indescribable ways. So, praise God today with expectant hearts.

My Memories

Moving to Idaho, we became members of a small community church. After twenty-three years at mega Saddleback Church in Southern California, it was quite a transition to one service attended by, on average, seventy people.

We quickly adapted to the smaller "family" feel of our new church, where we now enjoy something that was new to us in the beginning. The worship service includes a time of praise, prayer, and sharing, where people in the congregation can voice prayer requests, give updates of previous prayer requests, and offer praises. Then the elder leading this portion of the service prays aloud for all the voiced prayer requests and extends gratitude for the praises.

My husband is now an elder and he takes his turn at leading this special time of prayer and praise. Sometimes, the elder begins by asking for one-sentence praises from the congregation, and what a blessing it is to hear a community of believers publically praising the attributes of God. This precious worship reminds our church every Sunday morning of God's goodness!

Your Memories

Praise may already be a vibrant part of your prayer life. Do you remember when you first started praising God? Was it spontaneous or did you take a class at your church on praising God? In today's story, Becky Harling said her mentor helped her focus on praise during a difficult time. Sometimes we need a nudge, especially when we're indulging in a poor-me pity party.

Praise God for whoever mentored you in the past and ask God to continue bringing godly mentors into your life. Consider being a mentor to someone. Mentoring is a two-way relationship where both the mentor and mentee grow stronger in their faith together. You can read more about mentoring in Generation to Generation on page 235.

If praise has not been a regular part of your time with God, start listing your praises now. Begin by remembering when you accepted Christ as your Lord and Savior. Praise God for sending his Son Jesus to die for your sins. Praise him for the person, or people, who guided you in the process of turning your life over to Jesus. Now just keep on praising him!

Ways to Remember God's Goodness—
Thirty-Day Praise Challenge ....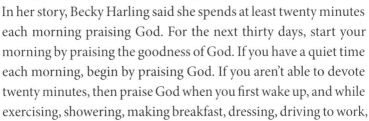

In her story, Becky Harling said she spends at least twenty minutes each morning praising God. For the next thirty days, start your morning by praising the goodness of God. If you have a quiet time each morning, begin by praising God. If you aren't able to devote twenty minutes, then praise God when you first wake up, and while exercising, showering, making breakfast, dressing, driving to work, getting the kids ready for school, working, washing the dishes, doing laundry or housework . . . whatever you do in the morning, and all day, acknowledge God. Notice the difference this makes in your day and write about it here. Why would you ever want to stop? Praise God even when you're not sure what he's doing in your life.

Let's Pray

Lord, you are so good and kind. Why do I always come to you with complaints and requests without stopping to thank and praise you for who you are, not just for what you do? Help me repent and praise you more. Wake me in the morning with praises on my lips before I face my day. I love you, Lord. I know you need to hear that more from me. Amen.

Talk about It

1. Do your prayers usually take the form of prayer requests—focused on you—or do you routinely offer praises to God—focused on his goodness? Which do you do the most?

2. Discuss the following praise Margaret Norris Kennedy shared on Facebook (reprinted here with permission). Which of the Ways to Remember God's Goodness that we've discussed so far can you find in Margaret's experience? Are you doing any of them yet?

Yesterday, I wrote in my journal from Psalm 34:8 to "Taste and see that The Lord is good." I promised The

Lord to proclaim publically his goodness as I saw it.
Plus, I asked him to manifest himself by accomplishing
a particular favor for me. At 6:00 P.M., he did the very
thing I asked him for. Now I am proclaiming to you the
goodness of The Lord.

3. Go through the alphabet praising a characteristic of God's goodness. I'll get you started:

A—Awesome. B—Benevolent. Now it's your turn to
continue through Z. When things aren't going your way,
remember this exercise and do it again!

4. If your church can't accommodate prayer and praise from the
congregation during a service, what other ways could they have
a time of public praise? In your Bible study or small group, spend
as much time praising God as you do petitioning him.

SECTION FOUR

CELEBRATING
GOD

*Feast there in the Presence of GOD, your God. Celebrate everything
that you and your families have accomplished under the blessing
of GOD, your God.*

—Deuteronomy 12:7 *The Message*

*Today, we would be celebrating my mother's one hundredth
birthday, so I wanted to slip away to the cemetery and write my
thoughts. My journals could fill pages of my memoir.*

—Jackie

God wanted the Israelites and their families to enjoy remembrance celebrations. Times of celebration afford us a great opportunity to look back at what was happening in our lives on previous birthdays, anniversaries, weddings, baby dedications, baptisms, family reunions, graduations . . . and to remember how good God has been to us in the subsequent years. Celebrating Easter, Thanksgiving, and Christmas reminds us of God's great sacrifice, provision, and love.

Chapter Fourteen

Celebrating His Renown

Your name, Lord, endures forever,
your renown, Lord, through all generations.

—Psalm 135:13

Our lives should be filled with such altars, monuments to the
goodness of God for how He has called and where He has led.

—Chris Tiegreen[1]

Bible Memories

Synonyms for renown are celebrity, fame, reputation, prominence, notoriety, stardom, and eminence. All of those certainly do apply to our Great God. Patriarchs of the faith built altars or memorials to commemorate God's renown and to remember making a sacrifice offering to God or having an encounter with him at a specific location. Altars were a permanent, public testament of worship and gratitude to God. For example, Abraham built altars of remembrance when he experienced a God-encounter.

The Lord appeared to Abram and said, "To your offspring I will give this land." So he built an altar there to the Lord, who had appeared to him. From there he went on toward the hills east of Bethel and pitched his

tent, with Bethel on the west and Ai on the east. There
he built an altar to the LORD and called on the name of
the LORD. (Gen. 12:7–8)

When Abram finally settled in the land God gave him, he built
another altar: "So Abram went to live near the great trees of Mamre
at Hebron, where he pitched his tents. There he built an altar to the
LORD" (Gen. 13:18). After Abraham (formerly Abram) resolved
a dispute with Abimelech over the ownership of a well on his
property, they resolved the issue with a covenant, and instead of
building a commemorative altar, "Abraham planted a tamarisk tree
in Beersheba, and there he called on the name of the LORD, the
Eternal God" (Gen. 21:33).

In Exodus 17:8–15, Joshua won a battle when Moses obeyed
God and held up his hands during the combat, with the help of
Aaron and Hur. Since Joshua and his army didn't see the unique
way God had helped them, "The LORD said to Moses, 'Write this
on a scroll as something to be remembered and make sure that
Joshua hears it.' . . . Moses built an altar and called it The LORD is
my Banner" (Exod. 17:14–15).

Other times, if they were traveling and didn't have time to
build a structure, the altar might be a mound of dirt or a pile of
stones to mark the spot where God intervened and helped them.

After Moses died, Joshua became the leader of the Israelites.
God commanded Joshua to take the people across the Jordan River
into the Promised Land, but it would be different this time:

And the LORD said to Joshua, "Today I will begin to
exalt you in the eyes of all Israel, so they may know that
I am with you as I was with Moses. Tell the priests who
carry the ark of the covenant: 'When you reach the edge
of the Jordan's waters, go and stand in the river.'" (Josh.
3:7–8)

God reminded Joshua of how he helped Moses safely cross the Red Sea, and that memory surely gave Joshua confidence that God would again perform a miracle at the Jordan River, which was at flood stage.

> Yet as soon as the priests who carried the ark reached the Jordan and their feet touched the water's edge, the water from upstream stopped flowing . . . while the water flowing down to the Sea of the Arabah (that is, the Dead Sea) was completely cut off. So the people crossed over opposite Jericho. The priests who carried the ark of the covenant of the LORD stopped in the middle of the Jordan and stood on dry ground, while all Israel passed by until the whole nation had completed the crossing on dry ground. . . . When the whole nation had finished crossing the Jordan, the LORD said to Joshua, "Choose twelve men from among the people, one from each tribe, and tell them to take up twelve stones from the middle of the Jordan, from right where the priests are standing, and carry them over with you and put them down at the place where you stay tonight." (Josh. 3:15b–17, 4:1–3)

Then God told Joshua to leave a remembrance altar of the twelve stones for future generations and "all the peoples of the earth" (4:24) to know the power of the Lord that again parted the waters for their safe crossing.

> In the future, when your children ask you, "What do these stones mean?" tell them that the flow of the Jordan was cut off before the ark of the covenant of the LORD. When it crossed the Jordan, the waters of the Jordan were cut off. These stones are to be a memorial to the people of Israel forever. (Josh. 4:6–7)

Then they celebrated.

> On the evening of the fourteenth day of the month,
> while camped at Gilgal on the plains of Jericho, the
> Israelites celebrated the Passover. The day after the
> Passover, that very day, they ate some of the produce
> of the land: unleavened bread and roasted grain. The
> manna stopped the day after they ate this food from the
> land; there was no longer any manna for the Israelites,
> but that year they ate the produce of Canaan. (Josh.
> 5:10–12)

The Israelites had witnessed God part the waters for their people not once, but twice! Then after years of eating the same food every single day, they now had fresh fruits and vegetables. The laughter and rejoicing surely reached to heaven.

Linda Remembers God's Goodness

When I lived in Orange County, California, Linda and I were walking buddies. We also became breast-cancer-survivor sisters and often celebrated together the way the Lord had restored our health. Just like God instructed Moses to build an altar and name it "The LORD is my Banner," Linda gives names to incidents or locations where something significant occurred—good or bad—as a reminder to celebrate and remember God's renown in that spot.

> A way that helps me remember the goodness of God is
> to name my incident or situation, or make a marker or
> title for the spot where I received healing or even injury.
> My neighbor recently inquired about my broken wrist.
> She had broken her wrist also, and she reminded me of
> how she curses the curb where she tripped every time
> she walks in that same area. I then told her I named
> the slope Angel Hill where I took a full-body, free-fall

face-plant. Whenever I walk down that hill or recall my fall, I remember God's faithfulness.

I explained that even though I took a hard fall, broke my wrist, hit my head, had facial abrasions, badly bruised my shoulder, bloodied both knees, and had a wrist and fingers swollen the size of small bananas, God's angels protected me: I didn't have a concussion. I didn't break or sprain an ankle or foot—no crutches—I could walk fine, and no surgery. Because of all these miracles, I still was able to travel with my husband to lead a mission team to Rwanda for two and a half weeks. Talk about miracles!

I've had health trials and God gloriously and faithfully restored my body. I want to tell everyone how grateful I am for his goodness. I'm always ready to share my story, and listen for opportunities to tell how God is active and alive in my life, guiding and protecting me. Even though in the world's eyes something looks like a negative—it's a great joy to commemorate and share the positive we can find in every situation.

My Memories

When Dave and I were first married, I dedicated several shelves in a hutch in our living room to commemorative memorabilia from our wedding: a wedding picture, the Bible I carried, a copy of the video, wedding gift candleholders, and our framed wedding invitation displayed on a picture stand. The invitation had a cross in the middle with a three-cord strand wrapped around it, and under the cross was Ecclesiastes 4:12, "A cord of three strands is not quickly broken."

My daughter commented it looked like a shrine. I explained that it was a visual reminder for us to celebrate our marriage and for everyone visiting our home to see that God is at the center of our marriage. As an anniversary gift, I framed our wedding vows, which hang on the wall in our bedroom. I never want us to forget the commitment we made to each other on our wedding day.

Marriage is a wonderful gift from God, so my husband and I also celebrate memories of our four children's weddings. We have a "hall of brides" with all of our wedding pictures displayed on a wall. Centerpieces or favors from each wedding decorate various areas in our home.

Our anniversary is December 19, only six days before Christmas; but we agreed to always celebrate, even get away for a few days, which we've done for twenty-three years!

Your Memories

What victorious occurrences in your life have you commemorated? Maybe you have a plaque or a framed picture in a prominent place, or you have named a spot where something memorable took place—good or bad. What memories flood your mind when you look at your "altar" or tell the story behind the name you gave the incident?

Ways to Remember God's Goodness—
Altars to God's Renown

The opening verse, Psalm 135:13, declares that God's renown will endure through all generations. We need to acknowledge God's renown in a way that lets our family and others know that we celebrate God in *every* area of our life. When something memorable happens, start looking for ways to commemorate and celebrate God's role in it. Here are some ideas.

- Give an occurrence or location of an incident a name that makes God the star.
- Create a visual such as a picture or keepsake that reminds you of how good God was in that incident or in a different situation.
- Save mementos. Start a scrapbook of special times to remember.
- Regularly review important documents that remind you of God's goodness and prominence in your life. For example: your wedding license, kids' birth certificates, final paperwork on your house or business, passports for a vacation, retirement, or mission trip.

What other ways can you think of to keep God center stage in your life?

keep scriptures posted where I can read them daily

Let's Pray

Abba, Father, you are Lord of Lord and King of Kings. You are the Creator of the universe and you always deserve to have the most prominent place in my life. Forgive me for the times I miss the opportunity to acknowledge you and share you with others. Help me look for you in everything and develop ways to make you the center of every area of my life. Amen.

Talk about It

1. Some churches still refer to an area at the front of the sanctuary as an altar, and an "altar call" is an invitation to come forward and pray to accept Jesus into your heart. Many modern-day churches have abandoned this tradition. After reading this chapter, what are your thoughts on how this shift away from "altars" might influence God's renown in the church today?

2. Look around your church. What banners or reminders do you see of God's renown? What is their meaning?

3. Where else in the world do you see banners or altars commemorating and remembering an incident? For example, there is the USS Arizona Memorial and the observance of Pearl Harbor Remembrance Day on December 7.

4. What must God think of the demolition, restriction, and banning by law of Christian celebrations, banners, and monuments? What effect has this disrespect for God had on our culture? How will it affect the next generation's remembrance of God?

Chapter Fifteen

Celebrating His Acts

Praise the LORD.
Praise God in his sanctuary;
praise him in his mighty heavens.
Praise him for his acts of power;
praise him for his surpassing greatness.

—Psalm 150:1–2

Broke the two thousand mark in my gratitude journal. Such a
simple yet powerful concept for remembering how good and kind
our God's acts are to us. Every item of gratitude gives me a fresh
perspective on life.

—Heidi McLaughlin

Bible Memories

God spoke to Moses through a burning bush to prepare him for
God's upcoming eminent acts: "I will stretch out My hand and
strike Egypt with all My miracles that I will perform in it. After that,
he will let you go. And I will give these people such favor in the sight
of the Egyptians that when you go, you will not go empty-handed"
(Exod. 3:20–21 HCSB). After their safe escape from Egypt, God told
the Israelites to celebrate his mighty acts performed on their behalf:

> Three times a year you are to celebrate a festival to me. Celebrate the Festival of Unleavened Bread; for seven days eat bread made without yeast, as I commanded you. Do this at the appointed time in the month of Aviv, for in that month you came out of Egypt. No one is to appear before me empty-handed. Celebrate the Festival of Harvest with the firstfruits of the crops you sow in your field. Celebrate the Festival of Ingathering at the end of the year, when you gather in your crops from the field. Three times a year all the men are to appear before the Sovereign LORD. (Exod. 23:14–17)

God knew that once the Israelites settled in the Promised Land, they would quickly forget all he had done for them unless they established annual celebration memorials. Regardless of the particular feast, it was a time to collectively remember and thank God for freeing them from Egypt during the Passover, the cost of that redemption, provision of crops and vineyards for food and sustenance, and the coming fulfillment of the prophets. The men were to lead their families in gratefully celebrating God's mighty acts of goodness toward them. The feasts and celebrations were a foretelling of the coming of Jesus—the fulfillment of the promises and prophecies.

- The Passover fulfilled in Christ's death (1 Cor. 5:7).
- The Festival of Firstfruits fulfilled in Christ's resurrection and the Holy Spirit coming at Pentecost (Acts 2).
- The Festival of Ingathering fulfilled by all those who accept Jesus as their Lord and Savior (Rev. 21:2–4).

For Christians saved by grace and the death and resurrection of Jesus, *every* day should be a day of celebration and thanksgiving of God's greatest act and sacrifice: "For God so loved the world that he gave his one and only Son, that whoever believes in him shall not perish but have eternal life" (John 3:16).

Jan Remembers God's Goodness

Jan suffered through two seasons of ovarian cancer, until after seven years of a valiant fight, she went to be with her precious Lord and Savior. Jan enlisted many rope holders, as she called her prayer team, and it was my privilege to be part of her team. Jan sent us frequent email updates of her cancer journey, and she always found acts of God to be thankful for and share from her Thankful List. Her rope holders celebrated victories with her, cried with her over bad reports, and prayed for her unceasingly.

Jan's Thankful List was in the thousands. Even on her worst days, she was still thankful for another day of life and praising God for his faithfulness and acts of love to her and her family. Before her passing, I asked Jan to share a few thoughts about her Thankful List.

Thanks so much for asking about my Thankful List . . . or Journal. Actually, I don't consider myself a journalist, but my thankful list has become pretty important, thanks to my daughter, Jill. When Ann Voskamp's *One Thousand Gifts* released, Jill gave me a copy. I was just facing recurrence number two of ovarian cancer, and she wanted me to read Ann's book. I understood and resonated with the premise of the book, *eucharisteo*, the act of giving thanks. Jill started writing her thankful list and kept asking when I was going to start writing mine, so I finally did.

When I'm down, discouraged, sad, or tired of the cancer/chemo routine, if I start adding to my thankful list, it doesn't take long before my focus is no longer on "poor me," but on celebrating the Lord and on how incredibly blessed I am. I can literally sense my spirit lifting into his presence. It's like a 180-degree turn-around. Amazing! Even when I think . . . *I can't think of ONE thing for which I'm thankful* . . . all I have to do is start writing, and then my mind is filled with tons of things for which I'm thankful.

I don't systematically reread all my lists, but I often thumb through the last few pages. Then I'm doubly thankful . . . the initial writing and remembering.

On my feel-good days, I try to write every day. Chemo days are the hardest, so I don't write. But once I begin to feel better, like today, I think back to the chemo days, remember, and record thankful things . . . God's provision of wonderful hydration nurses and maybe conversations we had with them or other patients.

Every night during Christmas, I write in my Thankful Journal, no matter how tired I am. Then when the decorations are down and packed away, I can still go to my journal, relive, and remember the many wonderful times we celebrated together as a family . . . popcorn balls, cutout cookies, the zoo, fishing in our backyard, visiting the manatees, and much more!

Jan's email updates and thankful list entries were an encouragement for whatever was happening in my life. I thought if Jan can still celebrate God's mighty acts while enduring horrific pain—even unto death—I can certainly do likewise.

Jan's family streamed a live celebration of her life so the rope holders around the world could participate and make comments online. There was camaraderie among those watching on our computers and those in the church in Florida. A community of rope holders celebrated the many lives touched by Jan and the mighty way God used her life and her love for people. A celebration none will soon forget.

My Memories

When my own cancer journey started, I became keenly aware of making memories with my family. At times like that, you think seriously about your mortality and the legacy you want to leave with your loved ones. You appreciate each new day of life. The sun rising every morning is an act of God to celebrate.

Holidays like Thanksgiving have new meaning. Typically, Thanksgiving is a celebration where family and friends gather for a feast, and everyone says what they're thankful for in the past year. But after finishing the dishes and putting away the leftovers, how many *really* remember what everyone said?

The Thanksgiving following my first breast cancer surgery, I had an idea of a Thankful Tablecloth. I purchased a Thanksgiving-themed tablecloth with plenty of white space and a box of wash-resistant colored markers. After Thanksgiving dinner, I brought out the markers and asked everyone—kids included—to find a spot on the tablecloth to write what they were thankful for that year, sign it, and date it. We traced handprints for the tiny ones with their name and age.

Today, we have years of thankful messages to read every Thanksgiving and remember the many acts of God's goodness to us and the people who joined us at the celebration table each year. If we go to someone's house for Thanksgiving dinner, I ask if I can bring our Thankful Tablecloth and markers.

When I go to be with the Lord, I pray my family will continue bringing out the Thankful Tablecloth as a reminder through the generations of how good God has been to our family and friends.

Your Memories

Have you celebrated accepting Jesus as your Lord and Savior? It was the most important, life-changing act of God in your life—or at least it should be. If you don't remember the exact place and time you asked Jesus into your heart, pray and ask God to remind you. Spend some time remembering things happening in your life at the time. Then arrive at a date to celebrate every year. It might not be the exact date, but it will be close enough. This is your eternal birthday—the day of your rebirth in Christ—so have a celebration party every year just like you would for your birthday and invite guests.

If you haven't made the commitment yet to follow Jesus, are you ready to do so now? I hope so. Go to the Salvation Prayer in the Appendix and pray to accept Jesus as your Lord and Savior. Then *today* is your spiritual birthday!

Ways to Remember God's Goodness—
Thankful List...

It's easy to overlook God's mighty acts—ones we might consider luck or take credit for ourselves. We need to learn how to celebrate the mighty acts of God more than once a year at Thanksgiving and view our life through the grid of perpetual gratefulness.

Journaling is an excellent way to acknowledge, record, and celebrate God at work in your daily life. You can find journaling tips in the Appendix. Many people recoil when they hear the word *journal*, but a thankful list like Jan's is less intimidating.

Most of us have to write to-do lists or have sticky notes in prominent places or we forget, even if it's important. I often forget my list after I write it, but writing it down embeds it in my memory. When I start to tell my husband things we need to do, he tells me to write them down for him.

You'll remember better what God does for you if at the end of each day you list three things you're thankful for, and then stop and praise God for allowing these occurrences in your life. If you're stumped, think about what life would be like without something you *do* have in your life. Or think of something you weren't expecting to happen that pleasantly surprised you. Thank God for being so present in your life.

After a week, read over your thankful list. Revisit your entries when a discouraging thought invades your mind or you're facing a challenge. If you notice your attitude improving while making this thankful list, continue with it—maybe not daily—but try making a list once a week and keep it in a spot you see often during the day. You'll never forget God's amazing acts of goodness if you develop an attitude of gratitude.

Let's Pray

Lord, thank you for saving my soul. Thank you for loving me. You are so good and worthy of my praise. I admit I don't celebrate you enough and thank you with appreciation for who you are, not just for what you do. Help me, Father, to remember that you show up each morning ready to guide my day—what an amazing act of devotion. I never want to forget how blessed I am to have you in my life every day, not just once a year. Help me learn how to live in an attitude of gratitude to you, Lord! Amen.

Talk about It

1. Describe a situation when you could have used rope holders like Jan had in her story (from Mark 2:1–5).

2. How has making a daily thankful list changed your attitude? How has it helped you remember to celebrate God's mighty acts in your life?

3. Thanksgiving is a day set aside to acknowledge and celebrate God's acts of kindness and provision to America. What could you do to put the focus more on God at Thanksgiving and less on feast and football?

4. When Jesus was on earth, he performed mighty acts and wonders, but the people still didn't believe in him, even in his hometown (Mark 6:1–5). Instead of celebrating him, they ran him out of town (Luke 4:28–30), and later crucified him. How can jubilantly celebrating Christ's acts in your daily life help others believe in him?

Chapter Sixteen

Celebrating His Name

I will come to you and bless you in every place where I cause My name to be remembered.

—Exodus 20:24b HCSB

My utmost goal in life is to portray Christ as best as I can and share the Good News that he offers to each and every one of us.

—Phil Robertson[1]

Bible Memories

When God instructed Moses to go to Pharaoh and tell this powerful ruler that he, Moses, was going to lead the Israelites out of Egypt, Moses questioned God:

> "Suppose I go to the Israelites and say to them, 'The God of your fathers has sent me to you,' and they ask me, 'What is his name?' Then what shall I tell them?"
>
> God said to Moses, "I AM WHO I AM. This is what you are to say to the Israelites: 'I AM has sent me to you.'"
>
> God also said to Moses, "Say to the Israelites, 'The LORD, the God of your fathers—the God of Abraham, the God of Isaac and the God of Jacob—has sent me to you.'

> "This is my name forever,
> the name you shall call me
> from generation to generation." (Exod. 3:13–15)

God was distinguishing himself from the plethora of Egyptian gods and idols with various names. The Egyptians even believed Pharaoh was the son of chief god Amon-Re. God told Moses that he would be known by I AM, which in Hebrew means "I will be"—a name reflecting God's dependable and faithful character and proof that God would fulfill his promises to free his people. A less formal name, the LORD (in Hebrew, *Yahweh*), means "He is" or "He will be." God speaks of himself as I AM and we speak of him as He is."

God will always orchestrate circumstances to make his name known and remembered. God warned Pharaoh, "For by now I could have stretched out my hand and struck you and your people with a plague that would have wiped you off the earth. But I have raised you up for this very purpose, that I might show you my power and that my name might be proclaimed in all the earth" (Exod. 9:15–16).

When Moses passed the leadership torch to Joshua, Moses gave the generation inheriting the Promised Land three sermons. In Deuteronomy 32, Moses follows God's previous instructions to change the message to a song: "Now write down this song and teach it to the Israelites and have them sing it" (Deut. 31:19a). Hearing something in a different format often makes it easier to remember. This song, a brief review of Israel's history, focuses on reminding the people of the previous generation's mistakes and warning the next generation to learn from those mistakes and not repeat their ancestors' disobedience to God. The song also offers hope in the name of the Lord: "I will proclaim the name of the LORD. Oh, praise the greatness of our God! He is the Rock, his works are perfect, and all his ways are just. A faithful God who does no wrong, upright and just is he" (Deut. 32:3–4).

Regardless of how often Moses preached, sang, prayed, and pleaded, or how many signs and wonders God performed, the Israelites remained a rebellious people for generations to come. They needed a Savior. They couldn't do right by God on their own.

Christmas celebrates the birth of that Savior—God's one and only Son came down to earth as a baby to save humanity: "And she will have a son, and you are to name him Jesus, for he will save his people from their sins. . . . Look! The virgin will conceive a child! She will give birth to a son, and they will call him Immanuel, which means 'God is with us'" (Matt. 1:21, 23 NLT).

Hebrew parents chose names with meaning and purpose for their children to fulfill, or to commemorate an occurrence during the child's birth. God named, or changed names of, individuals to reflect their purpose and role in his great plan. The name Jesus means the same in New Testament Greek as the Hebrew name Joshua—*God is salvation*. Joshua led the Israelites into the Promised Land, and Jesus would lead his people into eternal life.

During Jesus's ministry, he confirmed that he was God in the flesh by referring to himself as I AM, even at the risk of being stoned to death: "'Very truly I tell you,' Jesus answered, 'before Abraham was born, I am!'" (John 8:58).

At the end of Jesus's earthly ministry, the people praised him and recognized he was the long-awaited Messiah—God's salvation: "The crowds that went ahead of him [Jesus] and those that followed shouted, 'Hosanna to the Son of David!' 'Blessed is he who comes in the name of the Lord!' 'Hosanna in the highest heaven!'" (Matt. 21:9). But the following week, they were shocked when Jesus again claimed to be I AM:

Jesus fully realized all that was going to happen to him, so he stepped forward to meet them. "Who are you looking for?" he asked.

"Jesus the Nazarene," they replied.

> "I AM he," Jesus said. . . . As Jesus said, "I AM he," they all drew back and fell to the ground! (John 18:4–6 NLT)

After Jesus's arrest, the people quickly forgot the goodness Jesus had done in the name of the Lord: "'What shall I do, then, with Jesus who is called the Messiah?' Pilate asked. They all answered, 'Crucify him!'" (Matt. 27:22).

Sadly, they did crucify him, but three days later Jesus arose, and when he ascended to heaven, he left the Holy Spirit for the disciples and all those who believed in him. Believers who repent, ask for forgiveness, and accept Jesus Christ as their Lord and Savior have the *same* Holy Spirit dwelling in them that raised Jesus from the dead. Yes, *that* Spirit of God lives in you and me!

Never forget the spiritual power you have in the name of the Lord, as David told Goliath before he felled him with a single stone. "You come against me with sword and spear and javelin, but I come against you in the name of the LORD Almighty" (1 Sam. 17:45). One day, even unbelievers, agnostics, and atheists will bow to God's name:

> For there is no other God but me—a just God and a Savior—no, not one! Let all the world look to me for salvation! For I am God; there is no other. . . . for it is true—that every knee in all the world shall bow to me, and every tongue shall swear allegiance to my name. (Isa. 45:21b–23 TLB)

> Therefore, God elevated him to the place of highest honor and gave him the name above all other names, that at the name of Jesus every knee should bow, in heaven and on earth and under the earth, and every tongue declare that Jesus Christ is Lord, to the glory of God the Father. (Phil. 2:9–11 NLT)

My fellow Christians, this world is not our home; "our citizenship is in heaven" (Phil. 3:20). We are "aliens and strangers" in the world (1 Pet. 2:11 NASB). We must live lives worthy of our eternal nationality and family name—Christian—children of God, little Christs. Never be ashamed or intimidated to say the cherished name of Jesus, your Savior, because if you deny him, he will deny you (Matt. 10:33). Proudly bear and honor his name and your heritage: "Let us exalt his name together" (Ps. 34:3). Celebrate, serve, pray, and rejoice in the precious holy name of Jesus Christ: "And whatever you do, whether in word or deed, do it all in the name of the Lord Jesus" (Col. 3:17a).

Laurie Wilson Sargent Remembers God's Goodness

Birthdays are a time of celebration—God gave us life that day and our family gave us a name. As children, we had birthday parties honoring us. Our guests sang happy birthday to "_____" and inserted *our* name. We beamed while our parents clicked pictures to go into albums—maybe digital albums today—so we could remember each major milestone of our life. As we grow older, we tend to give less significance to our birthdays—often working or doing mundane adult tasks—and we don't always take time to celebrate the miracle of our birth. Laurie Wilson Sargent points out that someone remembering us by name on our birthday never gets old, no matter how old we get.

On my birthday a few years ago, I was doing ordinary chores: bed making, clearing counters, and cleaning bathrooms. If you're like me, you tend to feel a little above such chores on your special day. However, they still needed doing. I recall having a fleeting thought . . . *Does anyone remember it's my birthday today?* My husband had remembered, and I knew my grown kids would; but I pondered for a moment my place in this world.

As I moved books, papers, and miscellaneous items from my dresser so I could dust, I saw two pennies. One was face up, showing Lincoln's face. The other was face down and it looked odd.

It was an old Lincoln wheat penny, sometimes called a wheat back penny. I was curious about the age of the penny, so I grabbed my magnifying glass to get a better look.

The date was 1957. *My* birth year!

What were the odds of finding a penny minted the same year I was born, only moments after pondering God's purpose for my birth?

I've since learned they minted the Lincoln wheat pennies from 1909 to 1958. It's strange to think God knew I was to come into this world the same year of that particular penny and my name would be Laurie.

My Memories

I'm a visual person. I remember best the things I actually see. My husband asks me how I can remember names, places, dates, and details of my life, not to mention details of other people's lives. When I'm trying to remember a specific event or detail, I visualize where I was at the time or who was with me—I set the scene in my mind and often the details come alive. This is tremendous help as a writer. When someone says his or her name or tells me information, I visualize something about the person or the name to remember.

People feel cherished, worthy, and significant when you know their name, something special about them, and where you met. When the Woman to Woman Mentoring Ministry first started at Saddleback Church, many women joined whom I'd never met before. Later, when I would see them at church, I prayed and asked God to help me remember their names. God gave me ideas like associating their name with something I was familiar with or visualizing something about their story that related to their name. Sometimes, I would mentally go through the alphabet as I saw one of them approaching, and her name would pop into my mind when I reached the letter starting her name.

Praise God, I remembered the names of the first three hundred women who joined the ministry. It was a blessing to see the smile and surprise on their faces when I greeted them by name. They seemed to stand up a little taller and more confidently when they realized I made an effort to know them by name.

As the ministry grew into the thousands, I wasn't able to remember every woman by name, but I could remember faces and acknowledge I knew them. To God be the glory, and I acknowledge I can do nothing apart from him.

When I meet people for the first time, it doesn't bother me if they don't remember my *earthly* name, but I do want them to remember my *eternal* name. Often a conversation starter is, "What do you do?" My answer: "I'm a *Christian* author and speaker." They'll usually ask, "What do you write?" My reply: "*Christian* nonfiction," and then I name some titles. That can be a conversation stopper or starter when they ask, "What was your name again?"

Your Memories

Remember a time when someone forgot your name, called you by the wrong name, or didn't remember ever meeting you. How did it make you feel?

How did you feel when someone you didn't expect to know your name knew it? What can you do to remember the names of people you meet? Would any of the ways I mentioned help you?

Do you remember ever feeling embarrassed or afraid to say you were a Christian? How do you feel about that situation now? What are some ways to be bold, but not abrasive, about your faith?

Ways to Remember God's Goodness—
Throw a Birthday Party for Jesus ....

You hear the name Santa Claus often during the Christmas season, but how often do you hear the name above all names: Jesus? As Christians, we celebrate Jesus coming to earth as a baby, and sometime during the Christmas season, you'll hear the Christmas story read in church from Luke 1 and 2. But outside of church, do you remember to celebrate that Christmas is Jesus's birthday?

One way to remember that Christmas is all about Jesus is to have a birthday party for him. Invite family and friends and have the kids act out the manger scene, while someone reads the Christmas story from Luke. Set up a small manger in your home using straw or hay, a basket for a bed, stuffed animals, and a baby doll wrapped in a blanket. Place the manger near your Christmas tree as a visual reminder of the Reason for the Season.

For Jesus's birthday party, have a birthday cake or cupcakes with candles and sing happy birthday to Jesus. Give everyone a party favor representative of the true meaning of Christmas. For the highlight of the party, place a birthday-gift bag by the manger or under your Christmas tree. Make birthday cards for Jesus on the computer with the heading: "Happy Birthday, Jesus. This year

I give Jesus _____." Print out the cards on colored card stock. Give each guest a birthday card for Jesus as they arrive and advise them to pray about what they would like to give Jesus as a gift this year—maybe more time, energy, or praise—and instruct them to write their gift to Jesus on the birthday card. Someone's gift just might be to surrender his or her heart to Jesus!

Guests can sign their card or remain anonymous and place it in the birthday bag. On Christmas Eve, read the gifts and pray for each gift-giver to stay true to that intent.

I guarantee this will be a birthday party everyone remembers, and many of your guests will want to celebrate Jesus's birthday with their family and friends, too. Of course, wish everyone you see during December a Merry CHRISTmas.

Let's Pray

Lord, holy, holy, holy is your name. I never want to forget the greatness of your name and the reason you sent your Son Jesus Christ to earth on Christmas Day to bring me, and all believers, hope for eternal life with you in our permanent home in heaven. Help me focus on that miracle at Christmas and every day. Please don't let me ever hesitate to say your name but instead proudly proclaim to the world that I bear your name as a Christian. Forgive me for the times I didn't say your name. In the precious Holy Name of Jesus I pray. Amen.

Talk about It

1. Number three in the Ten Commandments is, "You shall not misuse the name of the LORD your God, for the LORD will not hold anyone guiltless who misuses his name" (Exod. 20:7). The *New King James Version* says, "You shall not take the name of the LORD your God in vain." How do you see the names of God and Jesus misused and taken in vain today? What is your response?

2. List the various biblical names of the Lord. For example, Redeemer, Savior . . .

3. What do you remember about your favorite birthday party? What made it so memorable?

4. How do you keep Jesus at the center of your Christmas? At the center of your life?

Chapter Seventeen

Celebrating His Blessings

The godly are showered with blessings.

—Proverbs 10:6a NLT

My blessing is this. I know a God who gives hope to the hopeless.
I know a God who loves the unlovable.
I know a God who comforts the sorrowful.
And I know a God who has planted this same power within me.
Within all of us. And for this blessing, may our response
always be, "Use me."

—Scott Dannemiller[1]

Bible Memories

Like the Israelites, we often measure God's blessings by what he does for us or gives us. And like them, we're seldom satisfied. When he gave the Israelites manna, they wanted meat. God gave them meat, but after gorging themselves, they were vomiting! He was ready to bless them with the Promised Land, but they were afraid of the giants. And so it went down through the generations. God wanted to bless them with heavenly treasures, but the people chose earthly kings and idols.

The Old Testament is a foretelling of Jesus, the blessing of the New Testament. Some words from the Old Testament have different meanings after the birth, death, and resurrection of Jesus. Theologian Dr. David A. DeWitt summarizes that transition regarding the word *blessings*: "In the Old Testament, the blessings of God were physical, earthly, and temporal, usually in the land of Israel. In the New Testament, the blessings of God were spiritual, heavenly, and eternal, not earthly prosperity."[2]

Jesus delineates his definition of blessings in the Sermon on the Mount in Matthew 5:1–12, the Beatitudes. His blessings may be the opposite of what you consider blessings. I call them the Great Reversal.

> Now when Jesus saw the crowds, he went up on a mountainside and sat down. His disciples came to him, and he began to teach them. He said:

> "Blessed are the poor in spirit, for theirs is the kingdom of heaven.
> Blessed are those who mourn, for they will be comforted.
> Blessed are the meek, for they will inherit the earth.
> Blessed are those who hunger and thirst for righteousness, for they will be filled.
> Blessed are the merciful, for they will be shown mercy.
> Blessed are the pure in heart, for they will see God.
> Blessed are the peacemakers, for they will be called children of God.
> Blessed are those who are persecuted because of righteousness, for theirs is the kingdom of heaven.

> "Blessed are you when people insult you, persecute you and falsely say all kinds of evil against you because of me. Rejoice and be glad, because great is your reward in

heaven, for in the same way they persecuted the prophets who were before you."

Some people do enjoy an abundance of material possessions and wealth, but that doesn't mean God blesses rich people more than he blesses people poor by earthly standards. God doesn't equate blessings with dollar signs. According to the Beatitudes and Jesus, prosperity theology is heretical. Blessings don't involve achieving, accomplishing, or acquiring.

God said there would always be poor among us, but he also said that *we* were the solution, and the blessing would fall on us when we "give generously to the poor, not grudgingly, for the LORD your God will bless you in everything you do" (Deut. 15:10 NLT). To whom God gives much, he expects much (Luke 12:48).

Millions of Christians around the world live each day on less than the minimum hourly wage in America, but they count themselves blessed because they know Jesus as their Savior and they're going to heaven. Now that's a blessing to celebrate!

Lindsey Bell Remembers God's Goodness

Lindsey Bell vulnerably shares the heartache of many women with secondary infertility. (It's one my stepdaughter shares in *Dear God, Why Can't I Have a Baby?*) But Lindsey learned how to celebrate the blessings she already had.

> Sometimes our problems grow so large in our eyes we can't see anything but them. That was me a couple of years ago. My husband and I, in a period of about two years, lost four babies to miscarriage. With each loss, my desire for a baby grew, and my brokenness became more and more pronounced.

I had two beautiful sons at home—one biological and one adopted. But my problem grew so big in my eyes, I couldn't see the blessings right in front of me.

God finally taught me that the cure for discontentment is not getting everything you want, but practicing gratitude for everything you have. As I began focusing on the blessings God already gave me, my problem began shrinking in my eyes.

The problem didn't go away, but it didn't consume my life as it had before. Now, even though God still hasn't fixed the issue and given me the child I long for, he has opened my eyes to the blessings I already have. On days when I start to get down, I look at my two children and remember to celebrate my blessings.

My Memories

When my husband Dave experienced his first layoff, I had just quit my job to start the Woman to Woman Mentoring Ministry as a lay ministry leader. We went from doing well financially to unemployment. Dave never went back into the corporate world and his next job had no benefits and low pay. Then he lost that job and took another labor-intensive, low-paying job.

During this time, the Woman to Woman Mentoring Ministry was spreading around the world as churches started the ministry for the women in their congregations. Thousands of women were experiencing the joys of walking side by side with Christ at the center of their mentoring relationships—and lives were changing. Dave and I both agreed you couldn't put a dollar value on those blessings.

At the time, my daughter Kim wasn't a believer and she couldn't understand why I wasn't receiving pay for leading the Mentoring Ministry at church. I tried to explain that money doesn't define ministry—a concept many believers still don't understand. While Dave and my earthly provision decreased, our heavenly blessings increased. We will never forget God's goodness in using us "About His Work," the name of my writing and speaking ministry. We were, and still are, blessed to be a blessing.

Your Memories

Have you had a tendency to think of blessings more in terms of acquiring things or financial windfalls or getting what you ask for in prayer? Those transient pseudo-blessings fade in our memory as quickly as the things wear out or break, the money is spent, or the next prayer request arises. Salvation, forgiveness of sin, and helping further God's kingdom are eternal blessings. Remember a time when you let God use you and you didn't receive anything material in return. Describe how that felt and label the experience a blessing.

Ways to Remember God's Goodness—
Count Your Blessings ....

Time yourself for two minutes and write down as many blessings as you can remember. Now look at that list and next to each blessing write: "I am" or "I could." *I am* using this blessing to further God's kingdom, or *I could* use this blessing to further God's kingdom. Pray about how to change "I could" to "I am."

Keep this blessing list in your Bible, and when you're having a down day, read and remember how very blessed you are to have Jesus in your life and to be used for his kingdom work.

Every Easter, remember to celebrate the incredible blessing of salvation: while you were still a sinner, Christ died a gruesome death on a cross, but he gloriously rose again three days later to bless you with eternal life forever with him. Nothing on earth can compare.

Let's Pray

Lord, thank you for opening my eyes to all the true blessings you bestow on me every day, and please help me to respond in a way worthy of those blessings. Use me to further your kingdom here on earth and help me keep the proper perspective of earthly versus eternal blessings. Teach me how to help others come to know the blessing of eternal life with you. Amen.

Talk about It

1. Read and discuss the words to the song "Count Your Blessings."[3] Now sing the song together with Guy Penrod Hymns.[4] (Links to lyrics and music are in endnotes.)

2. Compare your perception of blessings to the Beatitudes in Matthew 5:1–12. How can you apply them as Be-Me-Attitudes?

3. Discuss why persecution for your faith can be a blessing to celebrate.

4. How has your perception of God's goodness changed with this discussion of blessings?

Chapter Eighteen

Celebrating His Mercies and Forgiveness

But with you there is forgiveness,
so that we can, with reverence, serve you.

—Psalm 130:4

No one has ever offended any of us to the degree that Israel
offended God, yet God still brought about redemption for a
remnant purely out of His mercy and love.

—Chris Tiegreen[1]

Bible Memories

Moses reminded the Israelites that if they became corrupt and worshiped false gods when they entered into the Promised Land, God would destroy them and scatter any remnants. But Moses also assured them God is a merciful and forgiving God who never forgets his promises or the people who remember and return to him:

> But if from there you seek the LORD your God, you will find him if you seek him with all your heart and with all your soul. When you are in distress and all these things have happened to you, then in later days you will return to the LORD your God and obey him. For the LORD your God is a merciful God; he will not abandon or destroy

you or forget the covenant with your ancestors, which
he confirmed to them by oath. (Deut. 4:29–31)

Even though Israel continually rejected and rebelled against God
throughout the Old Testament, and today Israel and most Jews still
reject Jesus as the Messiah, God will have mercy on the remnant of
Jews who will someday believe. "So too, at the present time there
is a remnant chosen by grace" (Rom. 11:5). God is ready to forgive
anyone who turns from his or her wicked ways, and turns to him.

The obstinate, hard hearts of the early Jews opened the doors for
the Gentiles—everyone not of Jewish descent—to receive salvation.

What the people of Israel sought so earnestly they did
not obtain. The elect among them did, but the others
were hardened. . . . Again I ask: Did they stumble so as
to fall beyond recovery? Not at all! Rather, because of
their transgression, salvation has come to the Gentiles
to make Israel envious. But if their transgression means
riches for the world, and their loss means riches for the
Gentiles, how much greater riches will their full inclu-
sion bring! (Rom. 11: 7, 11–12)

Another word for Gentiles is pagan or heathen. You probably never
thought of yourself as a pagan or heathen, but you were, as is *every*
unbeliever. The Good News is that, thanks to the goodness and
mercy of God, salvation is available to *all* who believe in the birth,
death, and resurrection of his Son Jesus Christ and repent and ask
forgiveness for their sins.

Mercy is undeserved and unearned forgiveness, and *only* God's
grace saves us. We can't earn grace: "For it is by grace you have
been saved, through faith—and this is not from yourselves, it is
the gift of God" (Eph. 2:8). It's hard to imagine anyone rejecting
this gift—and it's not only the Jews—it's every atheist, agnostic, or
unbeliever who won't surrender his or her life to Jesus.

But a loving God who sent his one and only Son to earth to die on the cross is ready—right up to someone's last breath—to forgive and forget. He or she won't have enjoyed the blessings of the Christian life on earth, but God's mercy is available to everyone. God's mercy doesn't wipe away the consequences of sinful behavior, but he will help us endure the repercussions and make restitution when possible.

Today, there are Messianic Jews who have converted to Christianity and received God's forgiveness and mercy through the Messiah, Jesus—praise God! The apostle Paul was a Jew persecuting Christians when he literally *saw the light*, and not only converted to Christianity, but also became an evangelist for Christ. In Romans 11:25–32, Paul explains God's plan of mercy and grace:

> I do not want you to be ignorant of this mystery, brothers and sisters, so that you may not be conceited: Israel has experienced a hardening in part until the full number of the Gentiles has come in, and in this way all Israel will be saved. As it is written:
>
> > "The deliverer will come from Zion;
> > he will turn godlessness away from Jacob.
> > And this is my covenant with them
> > when I take away their sins."
>
> As far as the gospel is concerned, they are enemies for your sake; but as far as election is concerned, they are loved on account of the patriarchs, for God's gifts and his call are irrevocable. Just as you who were at one time disobedient to God have now received mercy as a result of their disobedience, so they too have now become disobedient in order that they too may now receive mercy as a result of God's mercy to you. For God has bound

everyone over to disobedience so that he may have mercy on them all.

Someday, God will turn the hearts of the Israelite remnant back to him and they'll recognize Jesus as their long-awaited Messiah; but when Jesus returns, those Israelites and nonbelievers who turn their back on God and his Son, will have lost their chance for salvation. Now is the hour to choose Jesus.

Nan Remembers God's Goodness

Nan knows the forgiveness, mercy, and free gift of grace the Lord offers to everyone who turns from his or her sinful ways and chooses to follow Jesus.

From ages seventeen to thirty-seven, I went about as low as you can go—without dying—into a promiscuous lifestyle. You name it, I did it. The more the merrier (I thought). My problem? Adventures, wrongful attractions, and getting-away-with-it syndromes. My parents were wonderful. No excuse there. I had a younger brother who was wise beyond his years, a dear friend. No excuse there.

So, from diet pills in high school and cut-up Vick's inhalers soaked in hot water from the lab class (yuck), I progressed through every other no-no, to heroin and cocaine.

Then my brother was saved in the Jesus-movement years of the seventies and he witnessed to me—actually led me to Christ—while I was on my way to Mexico to find peace. He sent me on my quest with a four-translation Bible and my promise to talk to, and read about,

Christ every day—but he knew I wasn't set free yet from my raw lifestyle.

I arrived in Santa Cruz, Mexico, to a dirt-floored room with an outhouse and many mango trees. I had no knowledge of what being saved or born-again meant. I just was both—thanks to my brother and the Spirit leading him. God caught me; I didn't know about me catching God.

So I did spend an hour each day learning about God. The other twenty-three hours were spent drunk, stoned, or both. Or walking over to the cow-lady for a quart of milk in this tiny village and grabbing a handful of freshly made tortillas at the tortilleria.

I wasn't there alone. Wally, my partner in crime, was a quadriplegic from a drug overdose. After a month, one morning we took a dose of LSD. A few hours later, I was standing at the glassless window watching a Mexican mother hang wet clothes on her fence across the dirt road with her three-year-old daughter helping. Watching them, I thought, *Sacheen is better off without me.* Sacheen was my little daughter, staying in California with my older sons.

Bam! That thought took root. I turned to Wally, who was laboriously typing poetry, and said, "We are better off dead, Wal. Let's commit a double suicide today. I don't have anything to live for and you don't either."

I could feel an attraction, of all things, to this idea. We batted it around for hours, me arguing for suicide and he being very quiet about it. I must have looked like a harridan as I screamed, "Let's DO it!" He looked me in the eye and said, with finality, "No."

"No? You mean, no?" Something I can only describe as a spiritual darkness left the room through the window, as a Light came into the room. I began feeling joy . . . a relief . . . I'd never known. "I don't have to die, Wally? I can live? I can live for my kids and be a Christian?" It was overwhelming. Wally was smiling and saying, "Yes!" His blue eyes beaming at my joy and wonder.

Completely delivered of drugs and darkness, we stayed up all night packing and caught a third-class bus the next day, with very little money in our pockets. Three days later, on the same Mexican bus with chickens, goats, his wheelchair, the blender, and the typewriter, we made it back to my brother in California to gather the kids, saying, "Come on, gang, we're going to be Christians now and go to church."

Wally and I were married and had two boys. Along with my daughter and the two older boys, we were a family. Life wasn't easy, but I finally had peace.

My Memories

I knew better. I had given my heart to the Lord at age eleven and lived a Christian lifestyle all through college, until I married an unbeliever and gradually began pulling away from God. I was on my way into the world and began making sinful choices when we divorced six years later. Choices I knew were wrong but still kept choosing.

The Lord left me in my wilderness for seventeen years, until finally I started to see the consequences of my worldly lifestyle—my young daughter was becoming just like me. It was a wakeup call that turned my life around. My Red Sea parted when I rededicated my life to the Lord at a Harvest Crusade after Pastor Greg Laurie asked the audience if they were ready to die tonight. I knew I wasn't, and I found myself on the stadium floor crying out to the Lord that his prodigal daughter had returned. When I left the crusade, the waters of my Red Sea closed behind me, burying my sinful past, and I walked out a free woman in Christ. It was six torturous years of daily praying before my sweet daughter experienced that same forgiveness and freedom in Christ.

God welcomed me back into his open arms and used a sinner like me to be About His Work in ministry. I choose not to focus on how far I fell away, but I will *always* remember his mercy and grace that lifted me back up into the Light from the depths of darkness.

Your Memories

Remind yourself of the mercies God has shown you over the years. Remember the times when you knew God forgave you, or was merciful, even though you were undeserving. Your good and gracious God who sent his Son to earth to die a terrible death for *your* redemption isn't going to abandon you now. When life gets tough—and it will—remember his past mercies and be encouraged.

If you are harboring a sin, or making wrong choices, take this time to repent before the Lord. Confess your sinful ways, ask for forgiveness, and pray for God's hand to guide you in leading a righteous life. Feel his peace invade your soul and remember the good, restful, and joyful feeling. That's how you should live *all* the time. Peace is not elusive. Losing peace is a red flag signaling something is wrong in your life. Come before the Lord with a repentant heart, ask for forgiveness, receive his mercy, and let God restore your joy.

Ways to Remember God's Goodness—
Taking Responsibility for Your Actions............ ✌

Fill in the blank: The person most responsible for my past transgressions is _____.

How did you fill in the blank? Common answers might be my parents, my spouse, God, the Devil, my friends . . . but these are just excuses. *Me* is the only correct answer. We always have a choice and are responsible and accountable for our decisions and actions—good or bad.

Mercifully, in spite of our wrong deeds and tendency to blame others, God still stands ready to forgive those who believe in him and ask for forgiveness. On a note card, write these words: God will forgive me, but I am responsible and will bear the consequences of my actions. Put this card in a place where you see it every day as a reminder that God offers forgiveness, but why do you want to do something he has to forgive? Why subject yourself to the repercussions of sinful behavior? Let the card remind you that sin is a choice, and *you* are ultimately responsible for your choices.

Remember that because of God's willingness to forgive your faults and failures, you can celebrate the person you are today—or the person you want to become.

Let's Pray

Lord, like everyone, I have gone astray and sinned. No one is perfect, only your Son, Jesus. Thank you for grace and unmerited favor . . . for your mercy in forgiving my past transgressions. Dwell in my heart and soul and help me make right choices pleasing to you. Purify me, Lord . . . I want to live a righteous life. Help me remember that as your child, I remain precious in your sight. Amen.

Talk about It

1. If you are a born-again Christian, God has forgiven you. Does remembering your own forgiveness help you forgive others? Should it? Why or why not?

2. Nan described feeling peace, and I described a welcome-home feeling in our stories in this chapter. What do you remember about how you felt when you first received God's merciful forgiveness and grace? How do you know God has forgiven you?

3. Kathy Howard admits there was a time when she "lost sight of God's sovereignty and grace. I traded my eternal perspective for an earthly one. But God faithfully refreshed my memory and called me back to Himself."[2] Describe a time when God refreshed your memory of his mercy and grace.

4. An acronym for grace is **G**od's **R**iches **A**t **C**hrist's **E**xpense. Discuss God's goodness in offering us grace instead of what we deserve as described in Ephesians 2:3–5:

> All of us also lived among them at one time, gratifying the cravings of our flesh and following its desires and thoughts. Like the rest, we were by nature deserving of wrath. But because of his great love for us, God, who is rich in mercy, made us alive with Christ even when we were dead in transgressions—it is by grace you have been saved.

SECTION FIVE

REMEMBERING GOD

You yourselves have seen what I did to Egypt, and how I carried you on eagles' wings and brought you to myself.

—Exodus 19:4

The key variable in receiving the goodness of God is the goodness of God.

—Chris Tiegreen[1]

Maybe you believe *intellectually* that God is good, but do you believe in your *heart* that you can trust him to be good to *you*? Do you worry that God's definition of good is different from your definition of good? Do you trust God's provision or your own efforts? Do you believe God has the power to fulfill his promises? Remembering God's goodness won't enhance your spiritual life until you fully *trust* God.

Chapter Nineteen

Remembering His Word

I seek you with all my heart;
do not let me stray from your commands.
I have hidden your word in my heart
that I might not sin against you.
Praise be to you, LORD;
teach me your decrees.

—Psalm 119:10–12

Unlike when we worry, when we meditate on God's Word, the
Bible tells us we are like a fruit bearing tree, planted by the water
(Psalm 1).

—Dr. David Stoop[1]

Bible Memories

After the death of Moses, God commissioned Joshua to lead the Israelites across the Jordan into the land God had promised them. An intimidating mission, but God and Moses had been grooming Joshua for such a time as this. God emphasized to Joshua the importance of carrying out this role by devotion to studying the Word of God given to Moses. Joshua was to read it, meditate on it, memorize it, and speak it aloud.

> Be strong and courageous, because you will lead these people to inherit the land I swore to their ancestors to give them. Be strong and very courageous. Be careful to obey all the law my servant Moses gave you; do not turn from it to the right or to the left, that you may be successful wherever you go. Keep this Book of the Law always on your lips; meditate on it day and night, so that you may be careful to do everything written in it. Then you will be prosperous and successful. Have I not commanded you? Be strong and courageous. Do not be afraid; do not be discouraged, for the LORD your God will be with you wherever you go. (Josh. 1:6–9)

David, who God said was a man after his own heart, wrote many psalms about meditating on God's Word and the importance of remembering in your heart what God says in the Bible. David may only have had access to the same five books of the Bible written by Moses that Joshua had—the Torah—to read and remember. Most people of David's time probably didn't have copies of the Torah or more likely couldn't read. One generation *spoke* the Torah to the next generation by memorizing and retelling it repeatedly down through the generations. Reading the Torah publically is part of Jewish communal life.

But sadly, the Israelites could not follow the law even though they knew it by heart. The prophet Jeremiah asked God why no one was wise enough to obey God and God answered him:

> Who is wise enough to understand this? Who has been instructed by the LORD and can explain it? Why has the land been ruined and laid waste like a desert that no one can cross?
>
> The LORD said, "It is because they have forsaken my law, which I set before them; they have not obeyed me or followed my law. Instead, they have followed the

stubbornness of their hearts; they have followed the Baals, as their ancestors taught them." (Jer. 9:12–14)

Today the Bible has sixty-six books, and few memorize the entire Bible, although I did have a professor in seminary who memorized the entire Gospel of Mark and recited it for us. Very impressive, but not something most of us aspire to emulate. However, having key verses readily available in our mind and heart in times of distress, praise, and decision-making reminds us of God's goodness and trustworthiness and helps us fend off the attacks of the evil one.

Today, Satan has deceived many who try to deceive others by twisting the Word of God to accommodate sin or declaring that the Bible doesn't apply to today's culture. What they call *irrelevant* God calls *irreverent*. Beware of these blasphemous arguments and their source. Since the Garden of Eden, Satan has entrapped and tempted many poor souls by treacherously planting the seed of doubt: "Did God really say . . . ?" R. C. Sproul Jr. describes what happens next when you bite into that apple:

> We begin by being embarrassed by portions of the Word of God. And we move to begin to massage the Word of God so that it starts to say the things that we want it to say. Soon we begin to move into ignoring the Word of God. . . . But because God speaks, because God will not be silenced, because when we push against the Word of God which is an immovable rock, sooner or later we will find ourselves cursing the Word of God, and spitting on it. . . . Friends, we can have our disagreements and discussions, but let us never ever speak of the Word of God as irrelevant letters from 2000 years ago.[2]

Culture doesn't define God's Word—God's Word defines culture. There's no replacement for reading and studying your Bible, but there are repercussions if you don't—you will starve and die spiritually and Satan will move in for the kill. Food sustains us *physically*; God's Word—the bread of life—sustains us *spiritually*.

> Jesus said to them, "Very truly I tell you, it is not Moses who has given you the bread from heaven, but it is my Father who gives you the true bread from heaven. For the bread of God is the bread that comes down from heaven and gives life to the world."
> "Sir," they said, "always give us this bread."
> Then Jesus declared, "I am the bread of life. Whoever comes to me will never go hungry, and whoever believes in me will never be thirsty. But as I told you, you have seen me and still you do not believe."
> (John 6:32–36)

Jesus is God's Word, the Bible—the Bread of Life—made flesh: "In the beginning the Word already existed. The Word was with God, and the Word was God. He existed in the beginning with God" (John 1:1–2 NLT). Even the Israelites were told "that man does not live on bread alone but on every word that comes from the mouth of the LORD" (Deut. 8:3b).

God instills in everyone a hunger for truth and righteousness. We can satisfy that hunger with spiritual food—the Word of God—and grow and mature in our Christian life and walk with Jesus. Or we can starve spiritually, fall victim to false teaching and unrighteous thinking, and walk with Satan. Feast or famine. Healthy or sickly. Nourished or malnourished. Courageous or weak. God's truth or Satan's lies. Satan preys on a dead spiritual life like a vulture preys on a dead animal. Choose Jesus. Read your Bible. Save your life!

Les Barnhart Remembers God's Goodness

Les Barnhart is the friend I told you about in the Preface who provided the inspiration for my writing this book. Les knows personally the courage and peace that accompany remembering God's Word and the terror of forgetting God's goodness. The Scripture Les had hidden in his heart replaced fear and trauma with faith and trust.

I have lived a life of doubts and lack of trust for most of my sixty-plus years. With the ebb and flow of life's experiences, I must confess, I've based most of my life on a short memory of God's faithfulness and vast provision. Experiencing a commission-based income all of my productive working years, I lived life expecting a vast free fall and fear of the what if's, rather than counting on God's safety net and perfect timing. With no recall of how good God has been to me, I opened myself to more victories for the evil one than for Jesus who has overcome the world. I am ashamed and disappointed in this behavior as a born-again believer since childhood.

Self-help books and weekly sermons from amazing Bible teachers didn't penetrate my inner man, until a Saturday morning in October 2010. I awoke that morning to a memory of a dream I had during the night. A dream laced with death, carnage, and calamity, but also with a Scripture reference, Psalm 27:3: "Though an army besiege me, my heart will not fear; though war break out against me, even then I will be confident."

For three years, I had been a defendant in a multi-million-dollar lawsuit consuming me with doubts, fears, and believing the worst was yet to come. My good character was under attack in unimaginable ways. I'd never had a dream referencing a Scripture before, but I knew without a doubt this was real and God was using it to get my attention. It was as though God were saying, *You are my beloved, I care for you. I am with you, do not fear, I am in control. Trust me.*

Twelve months later, I was the last to testify in what became a five-week jury trial. The years leading up to the trial, I envisioned—rehearsed in my mind—fear and intimidation in the courtroom. But Psalm 27:3 in my dream was God giving me advance assurance: *you are my child, you have nothing to fear.* As I walked into the courtroom to testify, I felt a boldness and empowerment I had never known.

At the conclusion of the trial, we waited seven long days for the jury to hand down a "not guilty" verdict for what became a landmark case. To God alone be the glory!

I now trust God that I can count on Jeremiah 29:11: "I have it all planned out—plans to take care of you, not abandon you, plans to give you the future you hope for" (*The Message*). *Amen!*

My Memories

I remember memorizing King James Version verses from my childhood Sunday school classes, and I love watching my grandchildren memorize Scripture. Admittedly, it's harder as I get older to memorize word for word, but I find that if I can remember the paraphrase or content of the Scripture from my daily Bible reading, it's easy to look up a key word in a concordance or an online Bible reference and find the entire Scripture.

It was a blessing to have the late Anne Ortlund, author of *Disciplines of a Beautiful Woman,* mentor me. One of the disciplines

Anne instilled in her mentees was reading the Bible cover to cover every year. That was over a decade ago, and I still start out every January reading the Bible in a year. I use various reading plans and different translations to provide variety and new insights into God's Word. I discover that every year I see the Scriptures in a fresh light reflective of the season of life I'm in at the time or the particular book I'm writing.

Reading and meditating on God's Word is my lifeline and a spiritual discipline I'm passing down to my children and grandchildren. As a former registered dietitian, I am passionate about my family's *physical* nourishment, but I am even more zealous about their *spiritual* nourishment.

Your Memories

What verses do you remember that spoke to you at a certain time in your life? Did you learn any Bible verses as a child that you remember today? If you can still recite them, congratulations! Now start learning some new ones.

Don't worry if you don't know or remember any Scriptures; you're never too old to make new memories. Choose a verse from the Bible that has special meaning to you. One that assures you of God's love and emphasizes that you can trust him. Write the verse on a note card and keep the note card with you until you have the verse and the reference memorized. Remember and recite the verse when you pray or journal or when facing a trial, temptation, or even tragedy.

Once you've mastered one verse, try another one. Your mind is like a muscle that will atrophy if you don't use it. Start with simple Scriptures and train your mind to remember the most valuable words you'll *ever* need to know this side of heaven.

Ways to Remember God's Goodness—
Reading the Bible .... ✐

If reading the Bible in a year seems intimidating, start at the Book of John and read the New Testament. Purchase a Bible highlighter (they don't bleed through the pages), and mark verses with special meaning to you or that you want to memorize.

My friend Barb says she has filled the margins in three One Year Bibles with daily notes about each day's reading and her life events at the time. Over the years, she has created a spiritual history of remembrances of God's goodness. Barb says, "Reading God's Holy Word daily and the events of the past I've written in the margins, both blessings and trials, remind me God is in control and his faithfulness never ends."

There are numerous tools available to help you read and study the Bible:

- YouVersion.com is an online reading program you can customize.
- Walk Thru the Bible has a monthly magazine providing commentary and life application discussion for daily reading.
- Some prefer the One Year Bible where you read a portion from the Old Testament, New Testament, Psalms, and Proverbs each day. Others like a study or life-application Bible with notes about the Scriptures.
- You can also listen to an audio Bible on your electronic device or in the car.
- There are many Bible translations. The Scriptures in this book are mostly *New International Version*, unless I indicated a different translation.

Whatever Bible reading plan or translation you choose, highlight in your Bible the words *remember, remembrance, reminder, never forget, forgot, forgotten, the next generation, forsake, and forsaken.* You'll quickly see that the Bible from Genesis to Revelation is a plea from God to remember the Trinity—God, his Son Jesus Christ, and the Holy Spirit—and to share the Christian lifestyle with the next generation. There's no right or wrong way to read the Bible—figure out what works for you and just do it!

Let's Pray

Father, help me to be disciplined about hiding your Word in my heart. Direct me to a way of reading, meditating, and studying my Bible that keeps me in your Word daily. Keep the evil one from making me think I don't have time, it's not important, I can skip it today, or I can't memorize Scripture. Help me remember that the sword of the Spirit, your Word in my mind and heart, is the only weapon I have against Satan's attacks. Guide me in how to stay true to your Word and not fall prey to false teaching. Thank you, Lord. Amen.

Talk about It

1. Discuss various ways you've found to memorize Scripture. Try memorizing a verse with another person and keep each other accountable for daily Bible reading.

2. Why do you think reading your Bible every day is so important? What would you need to change in your schedule to make that possible?

3. In his story, Les Barnhart's dream included a Scripture during a troubled time in his life. Why do you think Les recognized the Scripture?

4. List ways available today to have your Bible with you at *all* times.

Chapter Twenty

Remembering His Ways

*The LORD is righteous in all his ways
and faithful in all he does.*

—Psalm 145:17

*But I understand that blessings don't happen when I want them
to, they happen when they're supposed to. So we are going to keep
faith and keep fighting no matter what.*

—Bengals player Devon Stills,[1]
upon learning his four-year-old daughter, Leah, still has cancer

Bible Memories

We view circumstances through the lens of our life experiences and understanding. If we filter God's goodness through our definition and expectancy of goodness, then we only look for those things that represent goodness to us.

During Jesus's ministry, the people were expecting the Messiah to be a warrior king with great political power, who would leverage his strength and supremacy to usher in the kingdom of God. That was not Jesus's way and so the Pharisees and spiritual leaders of the day reasoned through their experience lens that Jesus could not possibly be the Messiah, even though they saw him heal the sick, raise the dead, cast out demons, and perform miracles. They were looking for something else—someone else.

The disciples also witnessed all of Jesus's miracles, including multiplying five loaves of bread and two fish into enough food to feed five thousand people with food left over (Mark 6:30–44), but still they were terrified at the way Jesus chose to rescue them when they were out at sea. It wasn't in their lens of experience, which most miracles aren't.

> Immediately [following the feeding of the five thousand] Jesus made his disciples get into the boat and go on ahead of him to Bethsaida, while he dismissed the crowd. After leaving them, he went up on a mountainside to pray.
>
> Later that night, the boat was in the middle of the lake, and he was alone on land. He saw the disciples straining at the oars, because the wind was against them. Shortly before dawn he went out to them, walking on the lake. He was about to pass by them, but when they saw him walking on the lake, they thought he was a ghost. They cried out, because they all saw him and were terrified. (Mark 6:45–50a)

They still didn't get it. In their terror, they forgot God's past goodness to them and to all the people he had just fed. "Immediately he spoke to them and said, 'Take courage! It is I. Don't be afraid.' Then he climbed into the boat with them, and the wind died down. They were completely amazed, for they had not understood about the loaves; their hearts were hardened" (Mark 6:50b–52). Just like Pharaoh's heart was hardened even though he too saw God demonstrate miraculous ways and wonders, it was not yet time for the disciples to understand Jesus's ways.

When they came to another setting where Jesus was teaching a group of four thousand who needed to be fed, his forgetful disciples again questioned, "But where in this remote place can anyone get enough bread to feed them?" (Mark 8:4). How could they have forgotten so quickly the feeding of the five thousand and Jesus walking on water? How could they forget what he was capable of doing?

We too can be *around* Jesus and yet *miss* Jesus. It's easy to fabricate Jesus into someone who makes us feel good instead of appreciating his goodness right in front of us, even when it hurts. Jesus knew the disciples didn't understand all that they saw, but he promised to leave someone who would help them remember him and his ways—the Holy Spirit.

> All this I have spoken while still with you. But the Advocate, the Holy Spirit, whom the Father will send in my name, will teach you all things and will remind you of everything I have said to you. Peace I leave with you; my peace I give you. I do not give to you as the world gives. Do not let your hearts be troubled and do not be afraid. (John 14:25–27)

Believers receive the Holy Spirit to remind us of God's goodness and help us honor his ways. Are you listening to the Holy Spirit, or are you still looking for a God of your own making who fits better into the lens of today's culture? Culture's ways won't last, but God's ways will last forever. God never stops being God.

Joanne Remembers God's Goodness

It's easy to recognize God's goodness when everything is going our way, but not so easy when he chooses a different way than the one we want, as Joanne experienced.

> It's not in the good times or when everything is going well, but in the trials or difficult times that I remember God's goodness the most. Sometimes I've seen his

goodness as he leads me through the trial; other times it's in the outcome.

One example began when I made an unwise marriage decision. I chose my stubborn way, not God's way. He patiently and lovingly watched and waited for the time when my life fell apart. Things started out good, but I eventually saw God's goodness in removing me from marriage to an unfaithful husband.

For the next five years, God taught me to depend on him for all my needs and those of my young children. He led me into the workplace where I could use and improve upon my limited clerical skills. He taught me to tithe my finances, time, and talents. I daily depended on him—something I might never have learned any other way. Eventually, he led me to a new faithful husband, and with our marriage, a blended family.

To remember the goodness of God, I have only to look at where I've been and where I am now. Lessons I'll remember, not just for the moment, but forever.

My Memories

When Dave and I were first married, we took a course from author and speaker Gary Smalley based on his book *Making Love Last Forever*. Gary encouraged couples to make memories as a couple and a family by doing activities, taking trips, and experiencing life together. Gary said the experiences we would remember and talk about the most would be the ones where things didn't go the way we planned. Those would be the stories we would tell over and over.

When people ask how Dave and I ended up in Idaho, it's a story that didn't go the way we expected. I thought Dave would work until his seventies and then we'd think about where we should retire. But surprise! Dave had to take an early medical retirement, and he prayerfully decided we needed to sell our home and move out of Southern California. At first, I said no way! I was a native Californian and not ready to make such a dramatic change; but it seemed like the only way, yet so different from our expectations of retirement.

So we sold our home and most of the contents, hired a mover, and relocated to the rural mountains of Idaho, where we didn't know anyone. Friends viewed us either sympathetically or longingly. I vacillated between apprehension and adventure.

I cried most of the road trip to Idaho. It was a huge transition. We still tell the story of feeling like Abraham and Sarah when God said pack up and move and they had no idea where they were going or why, and neither did we.

April 1, the day we moved into our new home, there was still snow on the ground, and the drizzling rain turned our dirt driveway into sloshy mud. The movers couldn't get the moving van up the steep, muddy driveway, so they carried all the boxes and furniture on their backs up the driveway and then removed their shoes before entering the house. I was praying all day for their safety. It made for quite a story.

Now we see the why in our move. We love our new church, new friends, new house, and the beauty of our mountain community. And best of all, Dave has become my helpmate and assistant in About His Work Ministries. For years, I pleaded with God for someone to help with the business side of the ministry and all the techie areas where I'm not gifted . . . I just never dreamed it would be Dave. But God knew all along—I just needed to get out of his way!

Your Memories

Remember a time when everything looked bleak and you wondered what God was doing; then you saw God do something that could only have happened his way. What did you learn from that experience and how did it stretch your faith? Make some notes so the next time you encounter difficulty, you'll pray for God to bring good out of it—his way.

Ways to Remember God's Goodness—
Being Bold about Your Faith............................ ✍

We live in a culture where vocal minority factions lobby to remove God from every public place, ceremony, and conversation. They reject God's ways, which can only mean accepting Satan's ways. There is no in-between—support God's ways or Satan's ways . . . the secular world's ways. The two will never meet or overlap—no straddling the fence between two polar opposites.

Christians, the silent majority for years in America, are watching our majority ranking decline due to passive apathy—letting a lost world lose God! Read the Gospels: Jesus wasn't silent or passive and he confronted sin and Satan! It's long past time for Christians to get noisy about the only right way—God's way. People say I'm bold about my faith and it surprises me that's considered an unusual trait . . . because shouldn't *every* Christian be bold? Our faith isn't a secret to hide; it's the answer to the world's woes. Unfortunately, Christians often worry more about offending the world than offending God.

Bold doesn't mean obnoxious. It simply means not being afraid to speak the truth, even in the face of adversity: "Therefore, since we have such a hope, we are very bold" (2 Cor. 3:12). Today's culture calls it unloving to confront untruths or lies, but that's a ploy of the enemy. The Bible says, "Love does not delight in evil but rejoices with the truth" (1 Cor. 13:6). Nothing could be more loving than helping someone find eternal life and freedom from the bondage of sin. Love without truth is cowardly. Truth without love is powerless.

As you boldly and lovingly share your faith and how God has showed you a way where there seemed to be no way, others will come to know the God you know. In the process, you'll remember the ways God has shown his goodness to you, even in the midst of difficult times.

Who do you know who is trying to straddle the fence between the world's ways and God's ways, or walk too close to the edge of temptation? Where has God been nudging you to be brave and bold about your faith? It will require getting out of your comfort zone, but comfortable isn't God's way. You won't be politically correct, but that wasn't Jesus's way.

Put a rubber band around your wrist to remind yourself that a rubber band only fulfills its purpose and usefulness when stretched. Where do you think God wants to stretch your faith? Pray about it and write down what the Holy Spirit brings to mind.

Let's Pray

Father, I often try to see you through an earthly viewpoint. Remind me that your ways are never going to be the world's ways. I want your way to be my way every day. Help me, Lord, to trust you more and accept that your ways are sometimes different from the way I think things should go. Teach me from my experiences so I can boldly share with a hurting world that you are a good God, all the time. Infuse me with boldness, but also kindness, so I can present my faith in a way others will receive and believe. And help me to live like I believe your ways are the only way. Amen.

Talk about It

1. Jesus's disciples repeatedly lacked trust, but it must have been devastating when his own mother and siblings didn't believe in him. Jesus's mother experienced divine conception (Luke 1:26–38) and praised the ways of God when she sang the Magnificat (Luke 1:46–55). But when Jesus began his ministry, she and his brothers thought he was crazy (Mark 3:20–21, 31–34). Discuss why Jesus's family lacked faith in him. How might you encounter some of the same issues in sharing your faith?

2. Discuss how the world's ways are different from God's ways in light of current news events.

3. What, if anything, holds you back from *completely* living in trust and faith in God's ways?

4. How will putting into practice some of the ways we've talked about remembering God's goodness help you become more cognizant of his ways in your life and the lives of others?

Chapter Twenty-One

Remembering His Love

I trust in God's unfailing love for ever and ever.

—Psalm 52:8b

God is a God of love. He loves you. He loves every one of us, and He loves us so much that He gave His Son to die on the cross. And when Jesus Christ was dying on the cross and shedding His blood, He was doing it for you.

—Billy Graham[1]

Bible Memories

One of the first verses we learn as children or new believers is John 3:16. This verse emphasizes how much God loves the world and wants everyone to have an opportunity to trust in him and his Son, Jesus Christ, and have eternal salvation. It's hard to imagine how anyone would turn down this kind of sacrificial love, but you and I both know people who don't accept God's love invitation. Sadly, they don't understand the consequences of rejecting God's love. *The Message* paraphrase of John 3:16–18 clearly states their fate:

> This is how much God loved the world: He gave his Son, his one and only Son. And this is why: so that no one need be destroyed; by believing in him, anyone can have

a whole and lasting life. God didn't go to all the trouble of sending his Son merely to point an accusing finger, telling the world how bad it was. He came to help, to put the world right again. Anyone who trusts in him is acquitted; anyone who refuses to trust him has long since been under the death sentence without knowing it. And why? Because of that person's failure to believe in the one-of-a-kind Son of God when introduced to him.

Loving God is a lifetime relationship. He never falls out of love with us; but believers who have fallen away from God, or who don't love him the way they did at first, are cautioned in Revelation 2:4–5 to remember and repent . . . or else.

But I have this [one charge to make] against you: that you have left (abandoned) the love that you had at first [you have deserted Me, your first love]. Remember then from what heights you have fallen. Repent (change the inner man to meet God's will) and do the works you did previously [when first you knew the Lord], or else I will visit you and remove your lampstand from its place, unless you change your mind *and* repent. (AMP)

Do you remember the zeal and excitement you had as a new believer? How grateful you were for salvation and Jesus's love and the intensity of your love for him . . . the thrill of feeling forgiven? You wanted to tell everyone about Jesus, until you realized not everyone was receptive to hearing about your new love. You became more cautious about sharing your faith for fear of rejection or ridicule. Your enthusiasm waned, and soon you didn't talk about Jesus unless you were with believers, and maybe not much then, either.

In the beginning of your faith walk, you had enthusiasm without knowledge. Don't let knowledge and time diminish enthusiasm.

Spiritual maturity should intensify adoration, not spawn complacency. Otherwise, your light will dim, as will your relationship with Christ, and you won't effectively share Christ's love with others. Remember, Jesus extinguishes lights that don't shine brightly for him (Rev. 2:5).

Michelle Lazurek Remembers God's Goodness

Michelle felt God's love through the actions of her church family. She learned God uses people who love him as a conduit of his love.

After many months of going to church and hanging around Christian friends, at eighteen years old, I gave my life to the Lord. I grew up in another faith, so I was accustomed to going to church, but I needed more. In May 1996, I got it. I remember this as one of the best days of my life, followed by several years of the worst days of my life.

My parents were strict followers of my former faith and disapproved of my Christian conversion. Many disagreements later, my parents came to my workplace and told me I wasn't welcome in their home. Devastated, I didn't know where to turn. Surrounded by black trash bags full of childhood memories, one thought crossed my mind: *I didn't sign up for this.*

During those years, it was hard enough to believe in God's existence, let alone his goodness. One particular night, deeply troubled with my current situation, I cried out to God, *Why are you doing this? What's happening? How could you allow this to happen to me?*

Feeling hopeless, I opened my Bible to Matthew 19:29: "And everyone who has left houses or brothers or sisters or father or mother or wife or children or fields for my sake will receive a hundred times as much and will inherit eternal life." Suddenly, I understood God had never left me. He was with me the whole time and would provide for me, no matter what my situation.

A short time later, a family from my church offered for me to stay with them rent-free in exchange for watching their children. People prayed for me, extended kind words, and gave money to help with my bills. With the kindness and love of my church family, God showed me his love and helped me remember his goodness.

My Memories

I can relate to Michelle's experience with her parents. My mother was a widow whose heart was hardened toward the Lord when my dad was murdered. When I became a Christian, she wanted no part of it. Later, when I didn't meet her expectations, she withheld love. I longed for my mother to experience the same unconditional love of Jesus I had found and for us to have a grace-filled, loving relationship. But my mother rejected every attempt at reconciliation.

In my family, love was given and taken away at will. I watched extended family members become estranged or disowned. It was a perilous, insecure way to live. I vowed that when I had children, I would love them no matter what they did.

When my daughter, Kim, was going through her prodigal years, she knew I didn't agree with her choices, but she also knew that didn't change my love for her. I didn't condone, but I didn't condemn. I know Kim never doubted my love. Now almost every birthday or Mother's Day card I receive contains these sentiments: "Thank you for being such a great mom and loving me unconditionally. I love you!"

Your Memories

Can you remember an occasion when someone loved you unconditionally, even when you weren't deserving of his or her love? What
did that feel like? If an infallible human being could love you that
way, surely an omniscient God could, too, don't you agree? Do you
believe God loves you unconditionally in spite of your imperfec-
tions? He does. How could you show that kind of love to someone
else? Take a few moments to write down who God brings to mind
and how he wants you to show love to that person.

Ways to Remember God's Goodness—
Write a Love Letter to God ....

You've probably written a love letter to show your affections for
someone you loved intensely. God's love for you is more passionate
and consuming than any earthly love, and he wrote a love letter to
you—the Bible. Your Bible is a love letter from beginning to end.
Know that love. Embrace it. Reciprocate it. God loves to hear from
his loved ones, too. So pray and ask God to remind you of all the
ways he's showered you with his love and then write him a love
letter from your heart.

Dear God,

Let's Pray

Dear heavenly Father, no one has, or ever will, love me with the same depth of love that you have shown me over and over. In spite of my actions and the many times I've disappointed you, God, you never withhold your love and you readily forgive my mishaps. How can I ever tell you how much I love you? Help me show your love to others and let them see your love light shining brightly in me. Amen.

Talk about It

1. In Michelle's story, and in my story, our parents didn't show us unconditional love. How does God define unconditional love in his Love Letter (1 Cor. 13:1–13)?

2. Even if our loved ones abandon us, who can we always trust to love us? (Hint: Psalm 27:10.)

3. Proverbs 17:17a says, "A friend loves at all times." How can we practice this?

4. How will remembering God's love for you help you to trust him more? Help you love others?

Chapter Twenty-Two

Remembering His Sacrifice

For Christ, our Passover lamb, has been sacrificed.

—1 Corinthians 5:7b

I poured the wine into the chalice our church had given me.
In the one-sixth gravity of the moon, the wine curled slowly and
gracefully up the side of the cup. . . . It was interesting to think that
the very first liquid ever poured on the moon, and the first food
eaten there, were communion elements.

—Edwin 'Buzz' Aldrin,[1]
    first man on the moon

Bible Memories

As Christians, we understand the extreme sacrifice God and Jesus endured: God gave his One and only Son, who became the last sacrificial lamb dying in atonement for our sins. Jesus died a painful and horrific death on a cross for you and for me. At Easter, we celebrate Jesus's resurrection three days later, and he lives today at the right hand of God—preparing a place for his followers who will someday join him in eternity. And he lives within the hearts of believers.

I don't know how we could ever forget such a sacrifice, but we do. The Israelites celebrated Passover to remember the night the angel of death passed over each home that had a sacrificial lamb's blood spread on the doorframe. They escaped from Egypt and were free thanks to Almighty God, and their children inherited a land flowing with milk and honey. But it wasn't long in the Promised Land before "everyone did what was right in their own eyes" (Judg. 17:6 ESV). Maybe they remembered the goodness of God ritually during Passover, but they lived sinful lives of idolatry and rebellion the rest of the time. "The Israelites did evil in the eyes of the LORD; they forgot the LORD their God and served the Baals and the Asherahs" (Judg. 3:7).

The law of the old covenant pointed out their sin, which they tried covering up with the blood of sacrificial animals on altars, but there was no heart change. They walked away the same sinful men and women. When God saw his people could not stop sinning—regardless of how often he disciplined and threatened them or how many animals they sacrificed—he sent Jesus and the grace of the new covenant.

Jesus's death on the cross would replace the sacrificial animal lamb with the sacrifice of the Lamb of God whose blood would wipe away their sins and change their hearts, and they would become new men and women in Christ: "You were dead because of your sins and because your sinful nature was not yet cut away. Then God made you alive with Christ, for he forgave all our sins. He canceled the record of the charges against us and took it away by nailing it to the cross" (Col. 2:13–14 NLT).

The night before his impending death, Jesus took his last Passover supper with his disciples: "So they prepared the Passover. When the hour came, Jesus and his apostles reclined at the table. And he said to them, 'I have eagerly desired to eat this Passover with you before I suffer. For I tell you, I will not eat it again until it finds fulfillment in the kingdom of God'" (Luke 22:13b–16).

Christ's last instructions to his disciples before going to the cross were to give thanks, take the bread and the wine, and *remember* him. Today we call this taking Communion or the Lord's Supper. In Greek, it is *Eucharistesas*, the heart of Christianity—to remember and to give thanks.

> After taking the cup, he gave thanks and said, "Take this and divide it among you. For I tell you I will not drink again from the fruit of the vine until the kingdom of God comes." And he took bread, gave thanks and broke it, and gave it to them, saying, "This is my body given for you; do this in remembrance of me." In the same way, after the supper he took the cup, saying, "This cup is the new covenant in my blood, which is poured out for you." (Luke 22:17–20)

Ann Voskamp, author of *One Thousand Gifts,* explains the significance of remembering and giving thanks during Communion:

> Isn't this what ultimately Christ asks of us in the Last Supper? One of the very last directives He offers to His disciples, the one of supreme import but I too often neglect: to remember. *Do this in remembrance of Me.* Remember and give thanks.
>
> This is the crux of Christianity: to remember and give thanks, *eucharisteo.*
>
> Why? Why is remembering and giving thanks the core of the Christ-faith? *Because remembering with thanks is what causes us to trust—to really believe.*
>
> All gratitude is ultimately gratitude for Christ, all remembering a remembrance of Him. For in Him all things were created, are sustained, have their being. Thus Christ is all there is to give thanks for; Christ is all there is to remember.[2]

The apostle Paul was not at the Last Supper with Jesus, but he knew its sacred meaning. In 1 Corinthians 11:17–34, he admonishes the

Corinthians that Communion was to be a lasting remembrance of Jesus's sacrifice; but the believers in Corinth had already forgotten the significance and were abusing it by bringing their own food and not sharing with the poor. Instead of commemorating a sacrifice, they were rude and selfish. Then Paul reminded them of Jesus's initiation of the Lord's Supper:

> For I received from the Lord what I also passed on to you: The Lord Jesus, on the night he was betrayed, took bread, and when he had given thanks, he broke it and said, "This is my body, which is for you; do this in remembrance of me." In the same way, after supper he took the cup, saying, "This cup is the new covenant in my blood; do this, whenever you drink it, in remembrance of me." For whenever you eat this bread and drink this cup, you proclaim the Lord's death until he comes. (1 Cor. 11:23–26)

Paul refreshed the believers' memories of the appropriate spiritual attitude prior to celebrating their freedom in Christ—examine your lives and be pure before God.

> So then, whoever eats the bread or drinks the cup of the Lord in an unworthy manner will be guilty of sinning against the body and blood of the Lord. Everyone ought to examine themselves before they eat of the bread and drink from the cup. For those who eat and drink without discerning the body of Christ eat and drink judgment on themselves. (1 Cor. 11:27–29)

Your pastor probably reads or recites these passages as you hold the bread and cup in your hand. Some churches take the elements of Communion together, and others instruct you to eat and drink on your own. Some serve the elements at the altar person by person, some serve row by row with the congregation seated, while others serve at a Communion table. God doesn't care when, where, or how you take Communion, as long as you do it with a clean heart in remembrance of Jesus and his sacrifice:

39 lashes
A crown of thorns
Hands and feet nailed to a cross
The 10,000 angels he could have called to rescue him
The world's sins he took on himself
Feeling forsaken
The torn veil
Shed blood
The final cry, "It is finished!"

Lisa Remembers God's Goodness

Lisa humbly admits that comparing ourselves with others or becoming preoccupied with the cares of the world can quickly replace the memories of Jesus's sacrificial love.

If you count complaining about current situations as forgetfulness, then yes, I forget. Just yesterday, I was thinking about a friend who I've witnessed to since junior high and how good her life is without Jesus. She has a beautiful house, a handsome boyfriend, and a successful career.

I was in a bad place yesterday, wondering why I even bother doing the right thing. I forgot about the peace that surpasses understanding I've felt over the years. I forgot strength beyond my means to take care of my dying mother. I forgot I was the girl my husband saw across a crowded room and had to meet. I just thought of the fancy car my friend drives and forgot my friend has also dealt with breast cancer, while I have not.

I forgot my sins, which drove nails into innocent hands and feet. God's been working on getting me back in focus.

My Memories

I've been in various churches that partake of Communion every week, every month, and once a quarter. I've helped serve and administer Communion, but my most memorable times of Communion are watching my grandchildren take the bread and juice. My heart swells with joy as each one commits his or her life to the Lord and celebrates Communion with parents and grandparents. It's a reminder of how spiritually blessed my husband and I are to be leaving a legacy of believers in the next generations. Praise God!

Your Memories

Do you remember your first celebration of the Lord's Supper— Communion? How did you feel? Were you excited? Humbled? Nervous? Confused? Grateful? You may have participated in Communion many times since, but try to recapture the newness and freshness of your first experience *every* time you take the elements.

Ways to Remember God's Goodness—
Taking Communion with a Thankful,
Repentant Heart .... ⌒

If you're not careful, you may take Communion as a ritual and tradition rather than a time of repentance and remembrance. It doesn't matter in what manner you take the elements, but what does matter is the condition of your heart. Before you partake in Communion, stop and remember what it signifies and why Christ had to go to the cross. Pray and give thanks to God for his goodness to care enough about you—yes, you—to offer you a way to be with him in heaven for eternity. Confess any recent sins and ask for forgiveness before chewing the bread or drinking the juice. You will never take Communion the same again. You will never forget the sacrifice.

When you pay your bills every month, remember the price Jesus paid to cancel your sin debt forever.

Let's Pray

Oh, Father, I'm so sorry my sins put you on that horrible cross. I cannot fully imagine the pain and horror you endured because of your love for sinful me. I know I'm unworthy and undeserving, but I want to spend the rest of my life honoring and remembering how much you love me. Thank you. Teach me to love you with all my heart, mind, soul, and strength. I worship and adore you. In remembrance of your Son, Jesus Christ. Amen.

Talk about It

1. Watch the movie *The Passion of the Christ* and discuss your heart's response to the gruesome cross scenes and what the sacrifice cost Jesus.

2. What painful sacrifice have you made for someone you loved? (Not necessarily physical pain.)

3. What painful sacrifice have you made for someone you didn't know, or maybe even like?

4. Take Communion together if you're in a group. If you're not in a group, take communion yourself; you don't have to be with others. Read and pray over 1 Corinthians 11:27–29 as you eat a cracker and drink a cup of juice in remembrance of Jesus Christ.

Chapter Twenty-Three

Remembering His Commission

And this is the testimony: God has given us eternal life, and this life is in his Son. Whoever has the Son has life; whoever does not have the Son of God does not have life.

—1 John 5:11–12

But as for me, how good it is to be near God!
I have made the Sovereign LORD my shelter,
and I will tell everyone about the wonderful things you do.

—Psalm 73:28 NLT

I find that as I share my story and my faith in God's goodness with others, it serves as a strong reminder to me as well.

—Christina

Bible Memories

There is no greater witness to God's goodness than sharing what he has done in your life. No one can question your testimony because it's your personal experience. Maybe you think the Great Commission is just for the disciples and pastors, but it's for *every* follower and believer of Jesus Christ. You don't have to be an evangelist to share your story.

God authorized and commanded me to commission
you: Go out and train everyone you meet, far and
near, in this way of life, marking them by baptism in
the threefold name: Father, Son, and Holy Spirit. Then
instruct them in the practice of all I have commanded
you. I'll be with you as you do this, day after day after
day, right up to the end of the age. (Matt. 28:18b–20
The Message)

Jesus told his disciples they would receive the Holy Spirit who
would help them testify about all they had witnessed during his
ministry on earth: "When the Advocate comes, whom I will send
to you from the Father—the Spirit of truth who goes out from
the Father—he will testify about me. And you also *must testify*,
for you have been with me from the beginning" (John 15:26–27;
emphasis added).

As we mature spiritually, we move beyond just remembering
God's goodness for our own benefit and start retelling our testimony to help others. You and I are Christians today because those
twelve disciples did just what Jesus instructed them to do. They
shared the gospel they had experienced with anyone who would
listen and with many who didn't listen.

We too receive the Advocate—the Holy Spirit—when we
become Christians, and our charge is the same as the disciples':
you *must testify* with everyone you meet.

You're here to be light, bringing out the God-colors in
the world. God is not a secret to be kept. We're going
public with this, as public as a city on a hill. If I make
you light-bearers, you don't think I'm going to hide
you under a bucket, do you? I'm putting you on a light
stand. Now that I've put you there on a hilltop, on a light
stand—shine! Keep open house; be generous with your
lives. By opening up to others, you'll prompt people

to open up with God, this generous Father in heaven. (Matt. 5:14–16 *The Message*)

Let's look at examples of two biblical testimonies. King Nebuchadnezzar is from the Old Testament and the apostle Paul is from the New Testament. They both wrote out their testimony recorded in the Bible, and they both humbly shared their testimony publically to influence others to trust in God's goodness. King Nebuchadnezzar shares in Daniel 4:

> To the nations and peoples of every language, who live in all the earth: May you prosper greatly! It is my pleasure to tell you about the miraculous signs and wonders that the Most High God has performed for me. How great are his signs, how mighty his wonders! His kingdom is an eternal kingdom; his dominion endures from generation to generation. I, Nebuchadnezzar, was at home in my palace, contented and prosperous. I had a dream that made me afraid. (Dan. 4:1–5a)

The king describes his dream to Daniel who interprets that the king's prideful attitude and wicked ways would result in him living like a wild animal and eating grass for seven years. The king admits ignoring Daniel's advice to repent, so then, "Twelve months later, as the king was walking on the roof of the royal palace of Babylon, he said, 'Is not this the great Babylon I have built as the royal residence, by my mighty power and for the glory of my majesty?'" (verses 29–30). At that moment, God fulfilled the king's dream and this mighty warrior king lived like a wild animal for seven years, until . . .

> At the end of that time, I, Nebuchadnezzar, raised my eyes toward heaven, and my sanity was restored. Then I praised the Most High; I honored and glorified him who lives forever. His dominion is an eternal dominion; his kingdom endures from generation to generation. . . . My

advisers and nobles sought me out, and I was restored to my throne and became even greater than before. Now I, Nebuchadnezzar, praise and exalt and glorify the King of heaven, because everything he does is right and all his ways are just. And those who walk in pride he is able to humble. (verses 34, 36–37)

Paul, formerly known as Saul, was a highly respected Jewish religious zealot proud of his persecution of Christians. On his way to Damascus to arrest Christians, he had an encounter with God. In Acts 22:1–16, Paul shares his testimony with a crowd:

"Brothers and fathers, listen now to my defense." When they heard him speak to them in Aramaic, they became very quiet. Then Paul said: "I am a Jew, born in Tarsus of Cilicia, but brought up in this city. I studied under Gamaliel and was thoroughly trained in the law of our ancestors. I was just as zealous for God as any of you are today. I persecuted the followers of this Way to their death, arresting both men and women and throwing them into prison, as the high priest and all the Council can themselves testify. I even obtained letters from them to their associates in Damascus, and went there to bring these people as prisoners to Jerusalem to be punished.

"About noon as I came near Damascus, suddenly a bright light from heaven flashed around me. I fell to the ground and heard a voice say to me, 'Saul! Saul! Why do you persecute me?'

"'Who are you, Lord?' I asked.

"'I am Jesus of Nazareth, whom you are persecuting,' he replied. My companions saw the light, but they did not understand the voice of him who was speaking to me.

"'What shall I do, Lord?' I asked.

"'Get up,' the Lord said, 'and go into Damascus.
There you will be told all that you have been assigned to
do.' My companions led me by the hand into Damascus,
because the brilliance of the light had blinded me.

"A man named Ananias came to see me. He was
a devout observer of the law and highly respected
by all the Jews living there. He stood beside me and
said, 'Brother Saul, receive your sight!' And at that very
moment I was able to see him.

"Then he said: 'The God of our ancestors has chosen
you to know his will and to see the Righteous One and
to hear words from his mouth. You will be his witness
to all people of what you have seen and heard. And now
what are you waiting for? Get up, be baptized and wash
your sins away, calling on his name.'"

King Nebuchadnezzar's and the apostle Paul's testimonies are
examples and encouragement that God can change anyone's heart:
once I was prideful, now I am humble. Once I was blind, now I see!

Wanda Remembers God's Goodness

In addition to our conversion testimony, we have testimonies of
God's goodness in life's experiences. When we tell our God stories, it reminds us of how good God has been to us. Here Wanda
testifies about her life-changing experiences of God's goodness to
encourage others.

In April 2002, I prayerfully walked away from a Vice
President's position with no replacement income. God
has cared for my household since that time. We have
most of our wants, and *all* of our needs. A month after
my work departure, I enrolled in the local Bible college.

I took classes and received a certificate for the teacher training track. Though I don't teach in a classroom, through God's goodness, I've had many opportunities to share my story as others witness my experiences.

Fast forward to 2008: four months after my husband lost his twenty-year position with a large company, I received a breast cancer diagnosis. God displayed his goodness on the day of my diagnosis. I went for a routine mammogram, requested a diagnostic mammogram, and left the Imaging Center four hours later knowing my future. During my treatment, I had opportunities to share spiritually with other women, and my family met all our financial needs and expenses throughout my cancer journey.

With God in my life, there is joy even in the midst of a storm—like the murder of my only son two years later. The outpouring of love, kindness, words, overwhelming financial support . . . was an ongoing testimony to God's faithfulness. God shows me every day how to participate in his earthly kingdom by using my hard places to help others see how he displays his goodness when we trust in him. It's my testimony.

My Memories

In earlier chapters, I shared my spiritual testimony that I accepted Christ as a young girl, and then spent seventeen wayward years after my divorce before rededicating my life to the Lord. In my life experience testimony, some of my testimony closely parallels Wanda's story. I, too, quit a high-paying job to go into full-time lay ministry and attend seminary. My husband went through a layoff three months after I left my job. A routine mammogram also diagnosed my breast cancer while my husband was experiencing another layoff, and my father was murdered when I was a child. Yet we both attest: I still believe. I still trust God. God is still good. That's our testimony to other women God puts in our paths who have had similar experiences.

I speak and write about these and other hard places as a witness that I could never have made it through any of them without God's help. People often comment on my transparency and openness, but I have nothing to hide. Others can't relate to me if I don't let them know I've experienced many of the same things as them; but praise God, he never stopped loving me and he never left my side—and I assure them he'll be there for them, too. Then they will have their own testimony to share of God's goodness.

We all have many varied testimonies in our life in addition to our salvation testimony. In Chapter One, I shared the Feed My Sheep story when God called me into ministry, and I tell that testimony often. God even allowed me to be the keynote speaker at the same Women in Ministry Conference where I heard God say, "Feed my sheep." It was their last conference, and as I told the audience about my initial encounter with God in the same room seven years prior, I felt a sense of commemoration—as if I were standing on holy ground.

When I share Feed My Sheep, I use stuffed animal sheep for a meaningful visual. Others also refer to my testimony as Feed My Sheep, and many give me toy stuffed sheep as a reminder of how my story touched them or how Woman to Woman Mentoring blessed the women of their church. I have flocks of stuffed sheep in my office, and when I look at one, I remember how good God was to choose me for the honor of helping women connect in Titus 2 mentoring relationships. I never tire of telling my story as HIStory.

My testimony also includes being a single, divorced, prodigal mom raising a prodigal daughter. When I told people I was writing *Praying for Your Prodigal Daughter* and would be including my daughter Kim's story, they often asked, "How does she feel about that?" Her answer . . .

> Mom, I want to share my story in your book because you also need my perspective. How can you effectively write about you and me if you don't know what I was feeling? You can't teach others what to do correctly if you don't know what works and doesn't work with kids. I'm so thankful I've come to know the Lord, that my life is so blessed, and that I didn't make too many serious mistakes along the way. If I can help you save one daughter by sharing my story, then that's what I want to do![1]

Today, it's a blessing to speak together and share our testimony. Watching my precious adult daughter eloquently share her prodigal journey as I share mine, I can only imagine how God is smiling down on us as we give hope and encouragement to other hurting parents and daughters.

Your Memories

Your spiritual journey is your testimony that describes your life before you turned it over—or returned—to God and how you've transformed into a new creation in Christ. Make some notes here to retrace that journey.

You may not think you have a testimony if you've been a Christian most of your life and life has gone smoothly for you. Well, that smooth life didn't just happen. God has been walking beside you guiding your life every step of the way. That's your testimony to others who worry about losing something by turning their lives over to God. You are a living example of how good God really is!

But if you have a hidden past you've been too embarrassed to talk about, now is the time to deal with those buried hurts and hang-ups. Just like all the stories and testimonies you've read in this book, God can use *every* experience for good, but not if we don't let him. The Bible tells us "the wages of sin is death" (Rom. 6:23), so hidden sin holds us in a death grip that silently destroys us spiritually, and often physically, from the inside out. Exposed sin loses its power. We don't have to waste energy and emotion worrying about others discovering our past. We can "thank God we've started listening to a new master, one whose commands set us free to live openly in *his* freedom!" (personalized from Rom. 6:18 *The Message*).

Is there a current sin or one from your past that God wants you to confess so he can use you to help someone else dealing with a similar sin? It takes courage, but he'll help you if you confess to him now and ask for forgiveness. Yes, it's embarrassing, but it's also freeing.

Think back to an experience where you know it had to be God who rescued you and how you might make that a testimony to his goodness.

Ways to Remember God's Goodness—
Share Your Story—Make It Your Testimony ...... ✓

Every time you give God the glory for something in your life, you testify to God's goodness. Your salvation testimony shares your life before Jesus, how he changed your heart, and how he spiritually saved your life. God has given you a story to share for his glory, so seize every opportunity to praise him and encourage others. I like this saying: sometimes God redeems your story by surrounding you with people who need to hear your past so it doesn't become their future. When we don't share *our* story, we don't share *his* story.

You must be willing to share how God helped you through difficult times, and that requires vulnerability, approachability, and responsibility. It's your witness to his faithfulness. It's the opportunity to give purpose to a crisis. Otherwise, you might spend your life feeling sorry for yourself—living as a victim instead of victorious. Revealing is the first step to healing.

Your story doesn't have to have a "happy ending" for you to share it. You give your testimony to show God's faithfulness *regardless* of the circumstances, and to assure others they're not alone or to stop someone else from making the same mistakes you did. Every day you encounter opportunities to share your testimony, and every time you tell it, you'll remember how good God has been to you. Let your loving heavenly Father guide you. Sometimes you'll only share a short snippet, and other times the whole story.

One of the steps in most recovery programs is publically telling your testimony to a group. Courageously sharing our past frees us from the death grip it had on us and opens the door to an unencumbered future. It also allows God to minister to someone in the audience going through something similar. Don't panic: you don't always have to share your testimony in a public setting. God will bring people across your path, and the Holy Spirit will prompt you to share one on one. When people ask me how I made it through life's difficulties, the best answer is, "I couldn't have done it without

God." And that's your best answer, too, and it opens the door to share your story.

Your story becomes *your testimony* when the focus is on God, not on you. Don't tell graphic details or anything to make someone else or you uncomfortable. It's not a tell-all, and it's not a time to tell someone else's story. Stick to details that pertain to you. Don't dramatize how bad you were; characterize how good God is!

When anyone tells me about an encounter with God, or a memorable circumstance in his or her life, I always ask if he or she is writing it down because God is going to use it as a life-experience testimony. We often forget details once the crisis or event is over, but keeping a record will refresh your memory when it's time to tell your story. You never know when the opportunity will arise, so be prepared.

If you haven't written out your spiritual testimony, do so now and use the notes you made after reading the Your Memories section. Think of it in five parts:

- Your life before Jesus.
- How, when, why you realized you needed a Savior.
- Making the commitment, or recommitment, and surrendering your life to Jesus.
- The change in your life since becoming a Christian.
- What being a Christian means to you.

In Psalm 71:15, the psalmist admits he's not sure if what he says will help, but he'll tell his story and let God choose how to use it: "My mouth will tell of your righteous deeds, of your saving acts all day long— though I know not how to relate them all." Some people may reject or rebuff your testimony. That's not a sign to stop telling it; you plant a seed, and God does the watering. Peter reminds us always to be ready to share our testimony.

> But in your hearts revere Christ as Lord. Always be prepared to give an answer to everyone who asks you to give the reason for the hope that you have. But do this with gentleness and respect, keeping a clear conscience, so that those who speak maliciously against your good behavior in Christ may be ashamed of their slander. (1 Pet. 3:15–16)

So don't worry about how God will use your testimony, or how someone will receive it. Just be willing to speak up when you feel the prompting of the Holy Spirit, and he'll use it for God's purpose. Sometimes it will be in a spiritual setting, other times when you least expect it. Be ready to share with or within . . .

- Church
- Bible study group or small group
- Mentoring relationships
- Others going through something similar
- Conversations acknowledging God's goodness in your daily life
- Social media
- Blogs
- Unbelievers or skeptics
- Support groups
- Where else?

What testimony does God want you to share and who needs to hear it? Who needs to know the reason for your hope?

Let's Pray

Dear Lord, thank you for giving me a testimony to tell of your faithfulness in all situations. Give me the courage and boldness to share my hard places as a reminder to me, and an encouragement to others, of the hope found in a life knowing and following you. Give me wisdom and discernment of what words and details to share discreetly and what to refrain from exposing. Use me, Lord, to expand your kingdom here on earth. Amen.

Talk about It

1. Share portions of your testimony. Tell when you accepted Christ as your personal Savior or depended on God to get you through a difficult time.

2. Challenge each other to look for opportunities to share your testimony. If you're not in a group, ask the Holy Spirit to prompt you to tell your testimony and ask a friend or family member to keep you accountable.

3. Discuss the potential power of your testimony.

4. How do we benefit when we allow God to use our mistakes to help others?

Generation
to Generation

Hear this, you elders;
listen, all who live in the land.
Has anything like this ever happened in your days
or in the days of your ancestors?
Tell it to your children, and let your children tell it to their children,
and their children to the next generation.

—Joel 1:2–3

When we think about what our churches are "leaving behind" for
our cities, we shouldn't be thinking of ministry plans or church
buildings, but kids. The children in our church are the first ones
that God has given us to win for the gospel. Because they are the
inheritance we are leaving for our city, the single most important
task we have as a church is to teach the next generation the gospel.

—Dr. J. D. Greear[1]

The Bible is a resounding call to remember God's goodness throughout all generations. It's a recorded history of our Christian faith reminding us *why* we believe and *what* we believe. Thanks to the saints who have gone before us, you and I have the privilege of reading the same Scriptures and biblical accounts our ancestors read. Now it's our job to ensure that God's unchanging Word prevails and reigns through future generations. We need to pass on the hope we have in Christ by equipping the next generation to read and understand the Bible and accept Jesus as their personal Savior—not encumber them with *rules* easily broken, but guide them toward a *relationship* they wouldn't forfeit or jeopardize for anything or anyone.

The Bible is a thread that intertwines us with previous generations who didn't have radios, television, smartphones, computers, Skype, Google Hangout, tablets, or even electricity. They heard Bible stories told to them or read the Bible by the fire or candlelight, the same Bible you and I read today. No other book in history has traversed the centuries, crossed cultures, and enjoyed such worldwide renown—even people who don't believe in God acknowledge the Bible is a historical book.

From the first writings of Moses in Genesis to the last recordings of John in Revelation—and every prophet, disciple, and apostle in between—there's a charge to remember God. Yet each writer knew we would have a propensity to forget God's words and forsake his ways unless one generation passed down the biblical truths to the next generation and lived out those truths. Paul voiced what every Christian should maintain, "Follow my example, as I follow the example of Christ" (1 Cor. 11:1).

It only takes one generation neglecting to pass down a heritage to the next generation for a way of life or belief system to vanish. That chilling fact underlines the magnitude of our responsibility to share the goodness of God with our children, grandchildren, and great grandchildren, and for them to do the same: "Direct your children onto the right path, and when they are older, they will not leave it" (Prov. 22:6 NLT).

The Israelites needed specific instructions to pass on God's truths to the next generation, or else when life was good in the Promised Land, that generation would soon forget everything God did in providing their good life. And we're no different today: looking for God to bail us out when times are tough and forgetting him when the good times roll.

God made sure the Israelites had a whale of a tale to tell to future generations. Before freeing the Israelites, God provided a platform to display his miraculous acts and wonders for a story too incredible not to share . . . and we still tell the story today:

> Then the LORD said to Moses, "Go to Pharaoh, for I have hardened his heart and the hearts of his officials so that I may perform these signs of mine among them that you may tell your children and grandchildren how I dealt harshly with the Egyptians and how I performed my signs among them, and that you may know that I am the LORD." (Exod. 10:1–2)

God specifically and repeatedly tells his people to pass down to future generations all the awesome wonders they saw him do because the younger generations weren't there. God even told Moses to preserve two quarts of manna for "the generations to come" so they would appreciate the unique way God fed their ancestors in the wilderness because manna would never flow from heaven again (Exod. 16:32–33). New generations didn't know God in the same personal, experiential sense as their parents and grandparents. "Remember today that your children were not the ones who saw and experienced the discipline of the LORD your God: his majesty, his mighty hand, his outstretched arm" (Deut. 11:2).

Telling family stories of God's goodness keeps the memories alive. We all have them; we need to share them with our children and grandchildren. Can't you just imagine the generation that came through the Red Sea on dry ground telling their wide-eyed grandkids sitting around the evening fire . . .

> Kids, you wouldn't believe it! The Egyptians took out after us in their chariots and horses, and we ran as fast as we could for days to escape them. But we all came to a screeching halt on the shores of the Red Sea. Trapped

between the Red Sea and the soldiers, we thought we
were goners for sure. We were terrified . . . screaming
and crying. But then, a miracle happened! God put a
cloud between the soldiers and us, and Moses raised his
staff over the sea and it parted right down the middle. I
mean, there was a dry path all the way to the other side!

The kids are oohing, aahing, wowing, and begging to hear more.
Great-grandpa chimes in,

Yes, sir. We thought we were dead for sure, but the next
thing you know we were all walking on dry ground to
the other shore. When the last person stepped on the
other side, the cloud lifted and the soldiers couldn't
believe what they saw. So they thought they'd be smart
and just follow us. We watched in awe as their horses
started getting confused and bucking them off. And
when they were all in the middle . . . the sea closed up
over them right before our eyes!

I tell you, kids, it was a miracle like none other. God
saved us and we were all free! We were cheering, singing, and on our knees praising God for his amazing
goodness to us. Be sure to tell your children and your
children's children about our incredible family legacy.

I'm sure the kids never tired of hearing that story, or the story of
Passover and how God spared everyone who had lamb's blood
over their doorframe, along with all the fascinating stories of the
journey in the wilderness. God wanted these stories told to future
generations, preserved forever. "This is a day you are to commemorate; for the generations to come you shall celebrate it as a festival
to the LORD—a lasting ordinance. . . . When you enter the land
that the LORD will give you as he promised, observe this ceremony.

And when your children ask you, 'What does this ceremony mean to you?' *then tell them . . .*" (Exod. 12:14, 25–27; emphasis added).

The first generation freed from Egypt would never see the Promised Land. An eleven-day journey took forty years because of their corrupt, disobedient, and rebellious behavior. So before dying, this generation also had to tell their children why they wouldn't be accompanying them. The kids and grandkids needed to understand the consequences of disobeying God.

When the time came for the adult children and their families to inherit the long-awaited land of milk and honey promised by God, Moses gave three sermons reminding them of all that transpired up to this point and why their ancestors weren't going to enjoy this blessing, not even Moses himself. Moses reads to them the Ten Commandments and warns them not to forget everything God did for their people once the hard times are a distant memory. "But watch out! Be careful never to forget what you yourself have seen. Do not let these memories escape from your mind as long as you live! And be sure to pass them on to your children and grandchildren" (Deut. 4:9 NLT).

Lastly, Moses reminded them of the greatest commandment of all:

> Love the LORD your God with all your heart and with all your soul and with all your strength. These commandments that I give you today are to be on your hearts. . . . Be careful that you do not forget the LORD, who brought you out of Egypt, out of the land of slavery. . . . In the future, when your son asks you, "What is the meaning of the stipulations, decrees and laws the LORD our God has commanded you?" *tell him.* . . . (Deut. 6:5–6, 12, 20–21a; emphasis added)

Sadly, they did forget once they settled in the Promised Land and their leaders, Joshua and the elders, died off. The younger generation hadn't made their parents' God their God: "After that whole generation had been gathered to their ancestors, another generation grew up who knew neither the LORD nor what he had done for Israel" (Judg. 2:10). As a result, "All the people did whatever seemed right in their own eyes" (Judg. 21:25b NLT). As in today's society, people abused the freedom to do whatever they wanted . . . whatever felt good and right to them.

Throughout the Bible, God warns and commands for the sake of each generation to pass down to the next generation the truths in his Word and his amazing goodness to all generations, so they would know him.

> My people, hear my teaching;
>> listen to the words of my mouth.
> I will open my mouth with a parable;
>> I will utter hidden things, things from of old—
> things we have heard and known,
>> things our ancestors have told us.
> We will not hide them from their descendants;
>> we will tell the next generation
> the praiseworthy deeds of the LORD,
>> his power, and the wonders he has done.
> He decreed statutes for Jacob
>> and established the law in Israel,
> which he commanded our ancestors
>> to teach their children,
> so the next generation would know them,
>> even the children yet to be born,
>> and they in turn would tell their children.
> Then they would put their trust in God
>> and would not forget his deeds
>> but would keep his commands.
> They would not be like their ancestors—

a stubborn and rebellious generation,
whose hearts were not loyal to God,
whose spirits were not faithful to him. (Ps. 78:1–8)

But each generation has become more and more lax in upholding, enforcing, and passing down God's truths. When I hear people lament about our corrupt world *today,* I encourage them to read the Bible. The truth is our world has been steadily deteriorating morally ever since Adam and Eve sinned in the Garden of Eden. Each generation pushes out the boundaries of sin and immorality a little further in the name of a progressive, tolerant culture. The twentieth century's sexual revolution has made sex outside of marriage, homosexuality, and abortion "acceptable." The twenty-first century's norm now becomes casual hookups, unwed pregnancies, transgenderism, gay marriage, gender change, and condoms passed out in schools. What one generation does in moderation, the next generation does in excess, and sadly that's been true since the beginning of time.

And why is sexual immorality worse than other sins? It violates God's holy temple—our bodies—created in his image, which is why he gives us these instructions:

Flee from sexual immorality. All other sins a person commits are outside the body, but whoever sins sexually, sins against their own body. Do you not know that your bodies are temples of the Holy Spirit, who is in you, whom you have received from God? You are not your own; you were bought at a price. Therefore honor God with your bodies. (1 Cor. 6:18–20)

We need to have these kinds of conversations straight from Scripture with our children and grandchildren. Remind them that God's ways *never* change, no matter the century—his ways are timeless and perfect and designed for our good, not our harm. Regardless of how people or government try to redefine or politicize morality, immorality *always* is detestable to God, as it should be to every Bible-believing Christian, and that's what we must share with the next generation.

There have been periods of revival in our history, usually at times when culture has sunk to an all-time moral low or there's a national crisis like 9/11. Suddenly, much of the world turns to God and begs his mercy and grace. As people flock to churches, unity and synergy bring communities together seeking God's peace and comfort. But when the shock deadens over the moral atrocity, like legalized abortion, or the crisis passes, the church attendance steadily decreases and the liberal agenda regains momentum. As a nation, we said we would never forget 9/11—as a culture, we did forget.

But our hope remains that, as bad as it is, God is still on his throne. Even though the world moves farther away from God, there are still people who will seek God, and we need to be ready to share the gospel with them. The church is not dead, but it needs to awaken from its slumber. As Christians, God calls us to live holy lives: separated *to* God, separated *from* the world, and separated *for* God. Our responsibility is to help a generation that thrives on conforming want to instead conform to God's standards! Don't think you can't make a difference. You can. Sure, you can't transform the *whole* world, but you can make a difference in *your* world.

Steve Green wrote a song with the chorus, "Oh, may all who come behind us find us faithful."[2] Someday we'll all just be a memory, but let's make sure that memory is a good one. In your sphere of influence, starting with your own family and church family, tell them everything you've seen God do and about his unchanging truths. Influence the next generations to love and obey God with born-again, Holy Spirit-filled hearts.

I pray my legacy to my children and grandchildren will be that Mom/Grammie was a woman who loved Jesus and lived what she believed.

Mentoring the Next Generation

Remember your leaders who taught you the word of God. Think of all the good that has come from their lives, and follow the example of their faith.

—Hebrews 13:7 NLT

I ask many Christian leaders, "What difference would it have made in your life if someone had come to you when you were twenty-one and offered to be your mentor and followed through on the offer?" The response is almost always accompanied by tears, and it almost always comes in the same words: "It would have made all the difference in the world!"

—Bobb Biehl[3]

Mentoring: Sharing Life's Experiences and God's Faithfulness

Each generation has a predisposition to look at God as the God of the past who doesn't understand the current culture. That's why I'm such a passionate proponent of mentoring and living out Titus 2:1–6, where spiritually older men and women receive the charge to teach, train, and model the Christian life to the next generation, so they won't be deceived and dissuaded. To understand the full impact of Titus 2:1–6, we need to read the issues Paul was addressing in the previous verses. It sounds a lot like our world today:

Everything is pure to those whose hearts are pure. But nothing is pure to those who are corrupt and unbelieving, because their minds and consciences are corrupted. Such people claim they know God, but they deny him by the way they live. They are detestable and disobedient, worthless for doing anything good. (Titus 1:15–16 NLT)

The next verses hold the apostle Paul's antidote for helping the next generation discern between fake professing Bible-bashing Christians, and true confessing Bible-believing Christians.

> *Your job* is to speak out on the things that make for solid doctrine. Guide older men into lives of temperance, dignity, and wisdom, into healthy faith, love, and endurance. Guide older women into lives of reverence so they end up as neither gossips nor drunks, but models of goodness. By looking at them, the younger women will know how to love their husbands and children, be virtuous and pure, keep a good house, be good wives. We don't want anyone looking down on God's Message because of their behavior. Also, guide the young men to live disciplined lives. (Titus 2:1–6 *The Message*, emphasis added)

Today we see a steady increase in crime and decrease in morality in our culture because many believers are failing to take up the Titus 2 mantle—one Paul and I call the job description for *every* Christian man and woman. A consequence of a generation *not* accepting the charge of Titus 2:1–6 is a liberal society aggressively challenging Christianity and long-held truths governing society for over two thousand years. Things were good; Christians ruled. Most people in our culture acknowledged God and lived by the Ten Commandments, but Christians got lazy.

We let the church teach our children and stopped caring beyond our own walls. The church failed to reach out to the next generation with a message relevant to the world they live in today, but the secular world was ready and waiting for them. The next generation is falling away from the church in droves or erroneously choosing a pseudo-gospel of compromise and feel-good theology. Today, even children from Bible-believing homes may not have the tools or fortitude to equip them to face a liberal world drifting away from the God of the Bible.

Living countercultural isn't easy and many children succumb to believing a fake gospel that seems easier and less confrontational. No one likes being the target of harassing name-calling: as intolerant, homophobic, old-fashioned, legalistic, or rigid. Even *conservative* is spewed with disdain. These kids are afraid to offend someone by talking about God or worry they won't have an answer when challenged as to why they're Christians.

It's no wonder they're confused and apprehensive. Satan is hijacking high-profile liberal pastors and several mainline denominations who expound that the Bible isn't inerrant or relevant, God is a myth, Jesus is a legend, and the church needs to catch up with the culture. Essentially, they're atheists trying to mask themselves as progressive Christians, as if they've discovered the true, open-minded Christianity that doesn't need the Bible. Wolves in sheep's clothing—straight out of Titus 1:15–16. Culture never trumps Scripture. Even if you've been a member for years of one of these denominations or churches that now succumbs to this unbiblical, satanical teaching—run—leave immediately, and take your family with you.

These liberal, misguided "teachers" defiantly ignore Jesus's warning that Christians are *in* the world, but not *of* the world. And Jesus didn't come to *conform* to the culture; he came to *reform* the culture. Jesus loves all people, but he hates sin—that's why he went to the cross. Not so we could keep on sinning, but because "the wages of sin is death, but the gift of God is eternal life in Christ Jesus our Lord" (Rom. 6:23). Whoever doesn't believe these truths cannot claim the cherished name of Christian, and Jesus has a message for them:

> If anyone causes one of these little ones—those who believe in me—to stumble, it would be better for them to have a large millstone hung around their neck and to be drowned in the depths of the sea. Woe to the world because of the things that cause people to stumble! Such things must come, but woe to the person through whom they come! (Matt. 18:6–7)

The next generation is vulnerable. Our children and grandchildren need parents, churches, and mentors not afraid to discuss openly and honestly the tough issues they encounter in the media, at school, and with their peers. The results of a survey, released March 2015, conducted by the nonpartisan Public Religion Research Institute of 2,314 adults aged eighteen to thirty-five—the millennial generation—are shocking and heartbreaking.

- Being *unaffiliated* with any religious tradition is the most common religious identity among this rising generation.
- When asked to make black-or-white moral judgments about sexuality, these young Americans will likely point out the gray.
- When it comes to sex, millennials don't always adhere to the rules of religious denominations, showing overwhelming support for the use of contraceptives.
- Eighty percent of young evangelicals say they've had premarital sex, according to a 2012 survey from the National Association of Evangelicals, and nearly one-third of this group's pregnancies end in abortion.
- On abortion, millennials' attitudes align closely with the attitudes of the general public.

- Despite religious denominations' attempts to tell millennials what a sexually healthy life looks like, most young Americans *do not go* to religious leaders for information about sex. They look to doctors, friends, and the Internet.[4]

Today's generation desperately needs help navigating the minefield of false doctrines and mistruths, even from those who call themselves pastors and evangelicals. Young people need to learn how to use the Bible as a benchmark to distinguish truth from lies. They don't need condoms and talks on safe sex; they need to know what to do when faced with inevitable temptations and how to make choices based on eternity, not just avoiding maternity.

Past generations welcomed the younger generation's help and mentored them as they worked side by side in the church, in the home, and at work. Today, the older generation often criticizes the younger generation's ways but refuses to teach and mentor them on the next generation's turf. Nowhere in Scripture does it say to take a hands-off approach and let the younger generation flounder and figure out things on their own. Instead, it says repeatedly that one generation is *responsible* for mentoring the next generation: "Remember the days of old; consider the generations long past. *Ask your father and he will tell you, your elders, and they will explain to you*"—some translations say "teach you" (Deut. 32:7; emphasis added).

We can't *ignore* the next generation's world of technology, music, and language; we can *influence* how they use it. To be influencers, we need to be aware and educated. They won't feel we don't understand their world if we *do* understand their world. We won't become *relics* if we stay *relevant*.

When we look at our liberal and godless world today, Christians have to accept much of the blame. How many are intentionally mentoring a spiritually younger woman or man or young person?

How many are making sure their children and grandchildren understand, accept, and embrace the Christian lifestyle? How many know, for certain, their children have a personal relationship with Jesus? How many feel a burden to pray for the salvation of their children and grandchildren? How many are ignoring the sins of this world, the sins of their children, and trying to twist Scripture to justify sin? How many are praying diligently for the younger generation?

Take heart . . . we have a godly legacy of greats to learn from who understood the value and rewards of mentoring the next generation.

- Moses trained Joshua in the ministry of leading the Israelites into the Promised Land.
- Ruth followed Naomi and wanted to know her God.
- Elijah mentored Elisha as his successor.
- Paul took Timothy as his spiritual son and attributed Timothy's faith to his grandmother Lois and his mother Eunice teaching him the Scriptures.
- Gabriel told Mary to go visit her elderly relative Elizabeth.
- Barnabas helped Paul mature spiritually.

Does your church take mentoring seriously? The next generation is crying out for moral direction and guidance. They need godly mentors and parents they can *respect* . . . and who they can *expect* to live out their faith. Hypocrisy—saying we believe in the Bible but not living by the Bible—will turn off children to Christianity at every age. Today's generation needs an authentic, spiritually wise older generation who will invest in the lives of those coming after them. They need mentors and parents to have the tough, honest discussions about abortion, sexuality, sexual exploitation, marriage, same-sex attraction, transgenderism, radical Islam, cults, drugs, alcohol, suicide . . . whatever they're facing in their world.

At best, the church has children for about one hundred hours a year. Parents have children for about eighty-five hundred waking hours a year. Home will always be the most fertile ground for children to see the Bible lived out in real life. If grandparents, parents, and the church don't mentor the next generation and help them set a godly moral compass, the world will eagerly fill the gap with a tolerant immoral compass. The next generation is looking for answers to the emptiness in their hearts that they're trying unsuccessfully to fill with drugs, alcohol, sex, alternate lifestyles, and, tragically, suicide. We have the answers they seek. We know what will fill that hole in their heart—Jesus Christ. Don't withhold this truth from them . . . their very lives, both physical and eternal, depend on someone sharing the Good News with them.

Dietrich Bonhoeffer, the German theologian and mentor whose Christian convictions cost him his life, talked about the relevance of mentoring and discipling the next generation to recognize the truth in his book *The Cost of Discipleship*:

> Cheap grace is the preaching of forgiveness without requiring repentance, baptism without church discipline, Communion without confession, absolution without personal confession. Cheap grace is grace without discipleship, grace without the cross, grace without Jesus Christ, living and incarnate.[5]

Bonhoeffer is a voice from a past generation mentoring future generations. Sadie Robertson is a seventeen-year-old voice from today's generation mentoring today's generation in her book *Live Original*:

> When you put your relationship with God first and you also have a great relationship with your family, you can risk having people get upset with you for standing up for your beliefs. You can risk being rejected because of

your values, and you can even risk losing a boyfriend if the relationship is not going in a godly direction. You can risk looking or acting different from other people. You can do these things because you know you will be okay without them. You know God is with you and for you, and I hope you can also know your family is standing beside you, but even without your family's support, you can know that God is there.[6]

Please join with me in a resounding *Amen.*

Ways to Implement Deuteronomy 6:6–9 with a Future Generation

Come, children, listen closely;
I'll give you a lesson in GOD worship.

—Psalm 34:11 *The Message*

Moses instructed the Israelites in how to pass on God's commandments to their children and grandchildren and make God a priority in their homes. It's wise counsel for us today, too.

These commandments that I give you today are to be on your hearts. Impress them on your children. Talk about them when you sit at home and when you walk along the road, when you lie down and when you get up. Tie them as symbols on your hands and bind them on your foreheads. Write them on the doorframes of your houses and on your gates. (Deut. 6:6–9)

Moses is describing how to make mentoring intentional in our homes—talk about God when you get up and when you lie down. When you walk with your children, eat with your children, play with your children, pray with and for your children . . . Think back over the last week: How often did you talk about God in your home?

These instructions were so vital that Moses emphasized them again in Deuteronomy 11:18–21. There is no greater challenge as a parent or grandparent than to teach your children and grandchildren the timeless truths of God's goodness. Lecturing is seldom effective, but role modeling and living out a godly daily life speaks volumes. The Christian life is more effective caught than taught. Show them that being a Christian is a daily way of life, not just on Sundays. Let them see you having quiet times with the Lord and reading your Bible. Remember, if you're reading the Bible on an electronic device, your kids don't know that. It looks to them like you're playing a game or checking social media or email.

Pray for your children and grandchildren *every* day and pray with them. You're not just helping them live a better life today, you're equipping them to be spiritual leaders of their generation and readying them for eternal life forever.

I remember sitting with my cousins on the floor around my Granny Reed's chair as she read Bible stories to us from her cherished, and well-worn, Bible. As I intentionally pass on the Christian faith to our grandchildren, I've found the following ideas effective for implementing Deuteronomy 6:6–9, and I hope they bless you, too. Engage their senses—children remember what they see, touch, taste, and feel.

These commandments that I give you today are to be on your hearts. Impress them on your children.

- Give children age-appropriate Bibles at an early age and show them how to read and study. If they can't read yet, read to them.
- Read to them from Christian storybooks when they are young, and give older kids Christian books to read. Discuss with them what they're reading.

- Choose gifts with a message: Christian board games, songs from Christian musicians, Bible character costumes and dress-up clothes.
- Take your children and grandchildren to church. Find a church they enjoy attending. Talk with them afterward about what they learned.
- Enroll young children in Awana, Vacation Bible School, children's Bible Study Fellowship, or other youth groups where they learn Scripture and read their Bible in a way fun for kids to learn.
- Introduce older children to church youth programs or ministries like Young Life, Youth for Christ, or Teen Challenge where they will grow in their faith with kids their own age.
- Choose Christian-based sports programs where they learn good sportsmanship and don't have games or practice on Sunday. Consider this: Is it more important for their eternal life for them to play in sports or grow in their faith? Find a sports program where they can do both.
- Teach them about quiet times and spending time with God each day reading their Bible and praying. Make sure you do this yourself for them to see and imitate.
- Tell family stories told for generations. Give your children a heritage to appreciate and remember.
- Look for teachable moments to apply God and his Word to their daily lives.
- Spend time with your kids and grandkids. Ask them about their dreams, ambitions, goals, friends . . . "What's God doing in your life?"
- Stay relevant in their world.

Talk about them when you sit at home and when you walk along the road, when you lie down and when you get up.

- Do age-appropriate Bible studies and daily devotionals together as a family.
- Pray as a family at meals, before school, at bedtime, and anytime there is a family issue or event—good or difficult. Invite children to take turns praying and praise them for a job well done. Pray before meals when eating out; otherwise, children will see prayer as embarrassing or only said in private.
- Use mealtime as a time to discuss God in their life. One woman says she has many Scriptures memorized because she had to recite a Scripture at dinner. I have jars with questions relating to the Christian way of life that my grandkids love to answer after we finish a meal. As they get older, there's another jar with Scriptures for them to look up in their Bibles and discuss.
- Bedtime is a great time to read a Bible story to discuss with the kids and pray together. Invite them to pray.
- When the children misbehave, show them a verse in the Bible that explains why this type of behavior is inappropriate and unpleasing to God.
- Discipline your children in love when they choose to do wrong or sin. Call sin "sin."
- Praise God with them for daily events such as: a good day at school, new friends, a good test grade, or feeling better after an illness.
- Play Christian music in your home, car, and electronic devices.
- Remember to talk about God so your children and grandchildren will remember God.

Tie them as symbols on your hands and bind them on your foreheads. Write them on the doorframes of your houses and on your gates.

The pious Jews literally did, and still do, attach small boxes called *mezuzahs* containing portions of Scripture to their foreheads, arms, and doorways. As Christians, discover creative ways to expose children to God's Word in their daily lives.

- We have a decorative Christian flag flying in front of our house to celebrate God in each season and holiday. Flying an American flag enforces a sense of patriotism.
- In our last home, we had a wrought iron dove, a symbol for the Holy Spirit, on our entry gate.
- We have a framed portrait of the Ten Commandments above our fireplace.
- Over doorways in our home, we have spiritual reminder plaques, such as: *Give us this day our daily bread. We put God first in the Thompson Family. Pray Always. Bless this home and all who enter. Christ the Unseen Guest in Every Room. FAITH is being sure of what you hope for.*
- I have a picture in my office of the youth camp where I accepted Christ as my Lord and Savior. A constant reminder of my salvation.
- When children are old enough to have electronic devices such as Kindles, tablets, iPads, cell phones, or computers, download a Bible app and show them how to use it. Send them Scripture texts and emails.

I'm sure you can come up with additional ways to help your family worship, honor, and remember God.

No time, you say? I think you would agree we all find time for what we value most. Helping your children embrace the Christian way of life is the best time investment you can make in your child's future. You are replaceable in every other area of life, but only *you* can be a godly mommy, daddy, grandma, or grandpa to your children and grandchildren. They are the future. They are the next generation who will influence the world, or be influenced, for or against God. May your children's heritage be that of Joshua's family: "But as for me and my household, we will serve the LORD" (Josh. 24:15b).

Talk about It

1. Who have you mentored and who is mentoring you?

2. Discuss why mentoring isn't as prevalent today as in former generations, and the ensuing repercussions. How would mentoring the next generation benefit today's culture?

3. How do you apply Deuteronomy 6:6–9 in your home?

4. Discuss the most valuable way you've discovered to remember the goodness of God.

Appendix

Journaling

This is what the LORD, the God of Israel, says:
"Write in a book all the words I have spoken to you."
—Jeremiah 30:2

Create a small "rescue" journal. Start today by writing down how
God shows up and answers your prayers. Every day add to your
journal. Each page—each entry—will increase your faith!
—Tricia Goyer

I mentioned earlier that when I was in the late Anne Ortlund's mentoring group, she had us read through the Bible in a year. We also journaled comments about each day's Bible reading and our prayers and praises. Anne wanted us to learn the spiritual discipline of journaling.

Another of Anne's stipulations was that when we completed our mentoring group with her, we start our own groups. When I told my Anne Ortlund mentoring group they would be journaling every day, there were universal groans, moans, and almost a mutiny. However, when the women started journaling, their attitudes quickly changed as they saw the value of recording God at work in their lives. Their journals became a tool for remembering God's goodness and increasing their faith.

Journaling is simply keeping a record of your life with the Lord. Now, who wouldn't want to do that! I prayed and journaled daily for six years for my prodigal daughter Kim. Over the years, it was easy to forget all the answers to prayer until I wrote the book *Praying for Your Prodigal Daughter* and reread journal entries such as, "I pray someday Kim will publically give her testimony." Today, Kim speaks with me in Two About His Work, and we share our testimony together. I might have forgotten I prayed about this had I not written it in my journal. I also journaled a prayer request for Kim and her father to reconcile, and they have. Because I kept a record of my journey praying for my daughter, I can offer hope and encouragement to other hurting parents.

Our memories are fallible. We won't remember everything we asked of God or how he answered. But we can assist our memories by jotting down reminders in the form of a journal. You don't have to be a writer to journal. Just a sentence or two will suffice. You have a Prayer and Praise Journal at the end of the Appendix, so you can start journaling today. Following are some tips to get you going.

Tips on Journaling

- Pray before you start.
- Select a journal that reflects your personality and style.
- Write your heart. Don't worry about grammar or sounding spiritual. Let your pen flow with thoughts and feelings.
- Think of journaling as writing a letter.
- Date your journal entries.
- Another way to experience journaling is as a chat or conversation. Freely write everything on your heart and mind. Prayer is simply talking or writing to God.
- If you want to write something confidential and worry someone might read your journal, develop abbreviations and symbols only you understand.

- You don't have to be upbeat. When it hurts, talk about it. When you're sad, cry out. When you're mad, it's okay. God can take it.
- Express the good and the bad.
- Journal during your quiet time or devotional time or right before you go to sleep.
- If you miss a day, don't worry about it. Just pick up the pen and start again. Maybe you'll only journal once a week.[1]

Combining Ways to Remember God's Goodness

My friend Charlene and I hope you find it helpful to read how she applies the following ways to remember God's goodness.

- Read your Bible daily.
- Memorize Scripture.
- Personalize Scripture.
- Study Scripture.
- Mentor others.
- Journal.

Charlene's Story

Our church enjoyed a sermon series on spiritual disciplines. Everyone nodded in agreement each week as we discussed prayer, Bible reading, and fasting. The Sunday morning the pastor announced journaling, the congregation burst into spontaneous laughter.

The practice of putting thoughts on paper has diminished as rapidly as the use of social networks has risen. The perception that "nobody does that anymore" may have motivated the congregation's laughter. Since I enjoy journaling, I was one of the few who didn't laugh. I started journaling along with Bible reading when I was in college. I'd use a simple Bible study method such as AEIOU—Ask questions, Examine words, Investigate, Other references, and Use it. Or Who, What, When, Where, and How. I became more familiar with the Bible and learned how to use reference tools including the concordance, commentaries, and Bible dictionaries.

Journaling continued to interest me through my adult years as I reflected on life changes and stages. What evolved was a spiritually enriching study sequence. A passage from a sermon or from personal Bible reading catches my attention. I read it in various translations along with any accompanying notes. Then I pray the Scripture, asking investigative questions. Finally, I journal a specific meditation.

For example, Isaiah 42:16 says, "I will lead the blind by ways they have not known, along unfamiliar paths I will guide them; I will turn the darkness into light before them and make the rough places smooth. These are the things I will do; I will not forsake them."

In praying the Scripture, I might say something like, "You will lead me as I travel new and unfamiliar paths. You will give me new insight where I can't yet see your plan. You will help me identify the obstacles to experiencing your will and prepare the way before me. Thank you for not abandoning me."

Investigative questions might be:

- In what ways am I blind to how God wants to work in my circumstances?
- What unfamiliar thing am I dealing with right now?
- What assurances do I need that God is at work in my circumstances?
- What obstacles do I need help overcoming?

Then I journal a personal meditation.

Isaiah 42:16 means you will not abandon me. Instead, you will . . .

- Guide me when I don't understand situations.
- Lead me when I need to do new things.
- Give me insight when I can't see the way.
- Present solutions when problems make things hard.
- You are my Servant King and I trust in you.

I call this process "writing back Scripture." I experienced the value of this process when I became a mentor to a colleague at work who confessed to having a drug problem. As I was praying Isaiah 42:16, remembering my meditation, I had a vision of my mentee walking along the unfamiliar path of rehabilitation. I developed a better understanding of the difficulties, which helped me pray for and mentor my mentee.

Laugh at the idea of journaling? Not me. I find it a valuable activity that draws me closer to God and increases my spiritual sensitivity. It's something I'll keep doing for as long as I can write.

Praying Scripture, as Charlene did, was essential when I was praying for my prodigal daughter, Kim. It kept me praying God's will for her, not just my will.

How Good Is God? You *Can* Remember . . .

In the Your Memories section in each chapter, you remembered how good God has been to you in the past as a reminder that he will *always* be good to you. On the computer or in a notebook, make three columns on a page with these headings:

God Has	God Is	God Will

Go back now and look at what you wrote for Your Memories in all twenty-three chapters, and under each heading list the ways you have seen God work in your life in the past (God Has); how God is working in your life in the present (God Is); and the promises you have read in Scripture (God Will).

When you finish, you should be secure in the fact that God is the same yesterday, today, and tomorrow. His goodness never changes.

Additional Ways to Remember God's Goodness

In each chapter, you read about a way to help you remember God's goodness and apply it to your spiritual life. Here are a few more, and I'm sure you can think of others.

- Listen to other people's testimonies and stories.
- Blog and share what God is doing in your life.
- Pay attention to sounds. Familiar sounds can help jog your memory to remember how good God was the last time you heard that sound. Garden waterfalls remind me of the tranquility I feel when I'm in harmony with God.
- Savor fragrances and smells. When I smell fried chicken, I remember my grandmother frying chicken for the family, which was her act of love and sacrifice for us since she was a vegetarian. In the Old Testament, the smell of burning sacrifices reminded the people of their covenant with God. Mary anointed Jesus before his death with perfume, and the fragrance filled the room. What smells remind you of times with God?
- Save emails, communication, or social networking discussions of God-incidents.
- Collect visuals. I mentioned I have stuffed sheep that remind me of my Feed My Sheep testimony. In Numbers 15:38–41, God told the Israelites to tie tassels on their

clothes so they would look at them and remember to obey God's commands. Maybe looking daily at your children, grandchildren, spouse, house, mementos, Bible . . . will be your reminder.

- Get out in nature or exercise. I often talk to God while I walk.
- What else?

Ten Truths to Remember about God

He speaks.
He is present.
He performs miracles.
He is faithful.
He is compassionate.
He answers prayer.
He forgives.
He believes in you.
He loves you.
He is good.

Taste and see that the LORD is good;
blessed is the one who takes refuge in him.

—Psalm 34:8

A Forever Prayer for You to Remember

Lord, I see your goodness in the past, which encourages me that you will be good in the present and in the future. I put my hope and trust in you. "For Jesus Christ is the same yesterday and today and forever" (Heb. 13:8). Amen.

A Salvation Prayer

Dear Jesus, I know I have sinned in my life, and I want to tell you how sorry I am. I ask you now to forgive me and cleanse me of those sins. Jesus, I want you to come into my heart and take residence there. I believe you are the Son of God and that you died on the cross to pay the price for my sins and then rose again in three days to offer me eternal life. Please fill me with the Holy Spirit and your love. Lord, I give you my life—make me a new creation in you. In Your Son Jesus's name I pray. Amen.

If you prayed the Salvation Prayer: Welcome to the family of God! God just wiped away your past sins and gave you a clean slate. You have been born again into a new life in Christ. Congratulations! Celebrate and tell others about the decision you just made to become a follower of Jesus Christ—it's your testimony. Now you're ready to grow and mature spiritually, and *Forsaken God?* will have so much more meaning to you.

Prayer and Praise Journal

Prayer Request	Praises

Prayer Request	Praises

Mentoring Relationships, Small Groups, and Book Club Guide

Forsaken God? is perfect to read and study together in a mentoring relationship or a group setting. Studies show we remember things longer if we talk about them, and it's helpful to get other people's insights.

For either a mentoring relationship or a group study, read a chapter between meetings and then get together to discuss the Talk about It discussion starters and questions at the end of each chapter.

Below, I have provided a sample format for group meetings. Select a discussion leader or rotate that privilege. The leader keeps the group on track and conversation flowing. There will be times of serious discussion, but allow time for some of the suggested activities to do together.

Support Group Guidelines

- Don't share personal information that would make you or someone else uncomfortable.
- Everything personal discussed in the group stays in the group.
- Make sure everyone has an opportunity to share, and one person doesn't dominate the time.
- This isn't a counseling session. It's okay to give tips and suggestions that have worked for you, but don't try to "fix" another person's situation.

- Prayer requests stay within the group unless given permission to ask others for prayer.

Suggested Group Format

- Open in prayer.
- Discuss and answer questions in the Talk about It section at the end of each chapter.
- Ask participants to name one or more things they gained from this chapter and how they will apply them to their lives.
- General discussion.
- Prayer requests.
- Fellowship.

About His Work Ministries

About His Work Ministries is Janet Thompson's writing and speaking ministry. Janet has an MA in Christian Leadership from Fuller Theological Seminary, and through her authored resources—*Woman to Woman Mentoring: How to Start, Grow, and Maintain a Mentoring Ministry* and the *Face-to-Face Bible Study Series*—thousands of women around the world enjoy the blessings and rewards of mentoring. Janet's passion is to equip men and women to practice Titus 2:1–6 and mentor the next generation in a lifestyle pleasing to God as they Share Life's Experiences and God's Faithfulness.

Janet is also the author of:

- *The Team That Jesus Built: How to Develop, Equip, and Commission a Women's Ministry Team*
- *Dear God, They Say It's Cancer: A Companion Guide for Women on the Breast Cancer Journey*
- *Dear God, Why Can't I Have a Baby? A Companion Guide for Couples on the Infertility Journey*
- *Dear God, He's Home! A Woman's Guide to Her Stay-at-Home Man*
- *Praying for Your Prodigal Daughter: Hope, Help & Encouragement for Hurting Parents*
- *God's Best for Your Life*

Two About His Work—Janet and her daughter Kim's conference and retreat speaking ministry.

Email: info@womantowomanmentoring.com
www.womantowomanmentoring.com
twitter.com/AHWministries
facebook.com/janetthompson.authorspeaker
pinterest.com/thompsonjanet

Notes

Preface
[1] Oswald Chambers, *My Utmost for His Highest*, updated edition, ed. James Reimann (Grand Rapids: Discovery House Publishers, 1995), February 11.
[2] Franklin Graham, Facebook timeline, February 24, 2015, http://tinyurl.com/kygo4vm.

Introduction
[1] Francis Chan, *Forgotten God* (Colorado Springs: David C. Cook, 2009), 33.
[2] Francis Chan, *Crazy Love* (Colorado Springs: David C. Cook, 2013), 44.

Section One
[1] Sarah Young, *Jesus Calling* (Nashville: Thomas Nelson, 2004), 29.

Chapter One
[1] A. W. Tozer, "The Speaking Voice," accessed March 30, 2015, http://www.the-highway.com/voice_Tozer.html.

Chapter Two
[1] Poppy Smith, *I'm Too Human to Be Like Jesus* (Living Parables, 2013), Kindle edition.

Chapter Three
[1] Chris Tiegreen, *The One Year Worship the King Devotional* (Carol Stream, IL: Tyndale House, 2008), 349.

Chapter Four
[1] Sarah Young, *Jesus Calling* (Nashville: Thomas Nelson, 2004), 360.

Section Two
[1] Rick Warren, *The Purpose Driven Life: What on Earth Am I Here For?* (Nashville: Thomas Nelson, 2013), 72.

Chapter Five
[1] Poppy Smith, *I'm Too Human to Be Like Jesus* (Living Parables, 2013), Kindle edition.

[2] Chris Tomlin, vocal performance of "How Great Is Our God," by Chris Tomlin, Christopher Dwayne Tomlin, Ed Cash, and Jesse Reeves, 2004, on *Arriving*, Sparrow Records.

Chapter Seven

[1] Ema McKinley with Cheryl Ricker, *Rush of Heaven: One Woman's Miraculous Encounter with Jesus* (Grand Rapids: Zondervan, 2014), 211.

Chapter Eight

[1] Rick Warren, *The Purpose Driven Life* (Grand Rapids: Zondervan, 2002), 18.

[2] Janet Thompson, *Dear God, They Say It's Cancer* (New York: Howard Books, a division of Simon & Schuster, 2006), 3.

[3] Warren, *The Purpose Driven Life*, 17.

Section Three

[1] Heidi Paulson, *Dependence Day* (Bloomington, IN: Crossbooks, 2010), 3–4.

Chapter Eleven

[1] Ema McKinley with Cheryl Ricker, *Rush of Heaven: One Woman's Miraculous Encounter with Jesus* (Grand Rapids: Zondervan, 2014), 215.

Chapter Twelve

[1] Chris Tiegreen, *The One Year Worship the King Devotional* (Carol Stream, IL: Tyndale House, 2008), 226.

Chapter Thirteen

[1] C. S. Lewis, *Reflections on the Psalms* (San Diego / New York / London: A Harvest Book / Harcourt, Inc., 1964), 95.

Chapter Fourteen

[1] Chris Tiegreen, *The One Year Worship the King Devotional* (Carol Stream, IL: Tyndale House, 2008), 336.

Chapter Sixteen

[1] Phil Robertson with Mark Schlabach, *UnPHILtered: The Way I See It* (New York: Howard Books, a division of Simon & Schuster, 2014), 3.

Chapter Seventeen

[1] Scott Dannemiller, "The One Thing Christians Should Stop Saying" *HuffPost Religion*, February 27, 2014, http://tinyurl.com/n8ckcmb.

[2] Dr. David A. DeWitt, "What It Means to Be Blessed by God," distributed by www.relationalconcepts.org, accessed March 31, 2015, http://tinyurl.com/o3q65ac.

[3] Johnson Oatman Jr. and Edwin Excell, "Count Your Blessings," *Songs for Young People* (Chicago, 1897), http://tinyurl.com/d9e4t46.

[4] Guy Penrod, "Count Your Blessings," *Hymns*, March 13, 2014, YouTube video, http://tinyurl.com/pht42be.

Chapter Eighteen

[1] Chris Tiegreen, *The One Year Worship the King Devotional* (Carol Stream, IL: Tyndale House, 2008), 147.

[2] Kathy Howard, "Flat Spots Here and There—Part 1," *Struggle to Victory* blog, April 23, 2013, http://tinyurl.com/q5swku9.

Section Five

[1] Chris Tiegreen, *The One Year Worship the King Devotional* (Carol Stream, IL: Tyndale House, 2008), 45.

Chapter Nineteen

[1] David Stoop, PhD, "Worry as a Form of Meditation," *Dr. David Stoop Devotionals* blog, February 17, 2015, http://tinyurl.com/pubcco4.

[2] R. C. Sproul Jr., "Rob Bell Not Faring Well," *Jesus Changes Everything* blog, February 18, 2015, http://tinyurl.com/o9hwza8.

Chapter Twenty

[1] Sydney Lupkin, "Devon Still's Heartbreaking Update on His Daughter's Cancer Battle," *Good Morning America*, January 13, 2015, http://tinyurl.com/qg7rl9c.

Chapter Twenty-One

[1] Billy Graham, "The Love of God," *Decision*, March 2015, 22.

Chapter Twenty-Two

[1] "Commoonion," *Snopes.com*, accessed March 31, 2015, www.snopes.com/glurge/communion.asp.

[2] Ann Voskamp, *One Thousand Gifts* (Grand Rapids: Zondervan, 2011), 153, 155.

Chapter Twenty-Three

[1] Janet Thompson, *Praying for Your Prodigal Daughter: Hope, Help & Encouragement for Hurting Parents* (New York: Howard Books, a division of Simon & Schuster, 2007), 303.

Generation to Generation

[1] J. D. Greear, "Two 'Gardens' God Uses to Grow Our Children," *Tabletalk*, March 2015, 39.

[2] Steve Green, vocal performance of "Find Us Faithful," by Jon Mohr, 1988, on *Hymns*, Birdwing Music/Jonathan Mark Music.

[3] Bobb Biehl, *Mentoring*, (Nashville: Broadman and Holman Publishers, 1996), 6.

[4] Carol Kuruvilla, "Millennials Want Contraception to Be Accessible to Everyone," *HuffPost Religion*, March 27, 2015, http://tinyurl.com/o83pjng.

[5] Dietrich Bonhoeffer, *The Cost of Discipleship* (New York: Touchstone, a division of Simon & Schuster, 1995), 44-45.

[6] Sadie Robertson with Beth Clark, *Live Original* (New York: Howard Books, a division of Simon & Schuster, 2007), 192.

Appendix

[1] Janet Thompson, *Dear God, They Say It's Cancer* (New York: Howard Books, a division of Simon & Schuster, 2006), 8 (adapted from).